Se__

Esteem

Overcome Insecurity And Boost Confidence
And Embrace Your True Self

*(Increase Your Social Skills And Improve Your
Emotional Intelligence To Gain More Mental
Control)*

Jennifer Heaton

Published By **Jessy Lindsay**

Jennifer Heaton

All Rights Reserved

*Overcome Insecurity And Boost Confidence
And Embrace Your True Self (Increase Your Social
Skills And Improve Your Emotional Intelligence To
Gain More Mental Control)*

ISBN 978-1-77485-559-1

No part of this guidebook shall be reproduced in any form without permission in writing from the publisher except in the case of brief quotations embodied in critical articles or reviews.

Legal & Disclaimer

The information contained in this ebook is not designed to replace or take the place of any form of medicine or professional medical advice. The information in this ebook has been provided for educational & entertainment purposes only.

The information contained in this book has been compiled from sources deemed reliable, and it is accurate to the best of the Author's knowledge; however, the Author cannot guarantee its accuracy and validity and cannot be held liable for any errors or omissions. Changes are periodically made to this book. You must consult your doctor or get professional medical advice before using any of the suggested remedies, techniques, or information in this book.

Table of contents

Introduction

This book provides practical steps and strategies for ways to boost confidence in yourself and self-esteem.

Find what makes you feel unhappy. Are you unhappy with your work? Are you single but would like to be engaged? Are you wishing you could have more friends to hang out with? What's stopping you from changing the things that make you feel unhappy? If you are in a position that they don't like or are afraid of going back to college to finish their education or even pursuing a different career. Someone who is having trouble making friends or to meet people may be stymied due to the fear.

While it's simple to recognize feelings such as worry or fear thatm are holding your back, the cause is a lack of confidence in yourself and self-esteem. If someone isn't confident in their own abilities and their abilities, they are likely to be reluctant to take on new challenges because they're unsure of the result. They are in their comfort zone , and they are unable to achieve anything more than what they currently have achieved in their life. They think they're at ease with being alone or they believe that their job is a good one therefore they don't need to do anything different.

A low self-esteem can also impact an individual's motivation to strive harder in their lives. Self-esteem is the measure of how people feel about themselves and the importance they give themselves. People with low self-esteem is likely to struggle in particular aspects of their lives. In the context of a relationship, for instance they might think that they are cheating on their partner because they don't believe they're worthy of the time of their partner.

In the course of reading this book, you'll be able to learn more about self-esteem and self-confidence and the effect each one of them has on your life. Additionally, you'll learn specific, concrete actions to enable you to achieve higher levels of each of these in your life, even as early as tomorrow.

Chapter 1: Believe In Yourself And Your Potential

In this life, we all face our own demons that we must confront and defeat. The most difficult part is taking the choice to stop the power of your demons. Your faith in yourself and in your capabilities is only half of the battle already won. If you keep on this track, with a firmness in your goals and conviction, you'll achieve your goals and the satisfaction you will feel that you get when you achieve it will be unimaginable.

Lack of confidence is usually due to having less or no faith in your capabilities and the worth of yourself. The majority of these negative feelings are brought on by external sources that break your confidence at every chance they receive. The more negative feedback comes about your actions or your opinions and the more hesitant you'll feel about speaking up to avoid being ridiculed yet again.

You must realize that the exact people who would like to tear you down and ridicule you are those who are afraid of your strength when you are at your best. They are aware of what you can do or are likely to be able of in the event that you freely display confidence in yourself. The bullies, if we can refer to them as such have their own thoughts of inadequacy that they project onto you. They transmit these negative feelings in hopes that you don't surpass them. They are their own demons to fight and defeat.

The earlier you can choose to put aside any negative thoughts and not worry about what other people are going to think or say, the more relaxed and confident be. Although it might be difficult, as simple as it seem, you must make an effort to erase off the thoughts of others from the equation and focus only about the goals you wish to accomplish and how it affects you. It will be apparent that you speak out more frequently on topics that you are knowledgeable about and you'll begin to be more confident in expressing your own views and defending your beliefs. Things will become easier and you'll be inclined to tackle them confident in the knowledge that in the event that you fail regardless of what other people think You just have to keep striving until

4

you achieve. Your confidence will increase and your anxiety will diminish each minute, and with each completed task you will be able to see the immense potential you have.

Confidence isn't something you can teach it's more of an inner awakening and an understanding that you are valued more than what you believe in and that your ideas and ideas are valuable regardless of the circumstance. If you feel inadequate and doesn't believe in their own abilities, it could be a very difficult situation to get out of but it is one that the chains must be removed for you to move forward and become your potential self. made to be.

This isn't something that can be changed over night, but more of a continuous work in the process of improvement. There are little, easy things you can do every day to get in a good mindset and ready to tackle the day ahead.

Relax in the morning as you get up, and fill your mind with positive thoughts. You can remind yourself of how gifted and unique you are, and how you have many gifts to share with the world.

Write down the things you'd like to do and get started and as you gain confidence in the small tasks and the bigger ones come easily.

Take care to show gratitude for those who express their opinion or accomplish tasks , as they may need an increase in their confidence and faith in their capabilities. It is likely that this attitude is contagious and others around you will soon be doing the similar thing. Perhaps your adversary will turn out to help you.

Be aware of and grateful for your strengths, even if they might not be apparent to the world at this point, you are aware of where your personal strengths are and have just wanted to get the right moment to reveal the world on your secrets.

Forgive those who want to dominate you and obscure your excellence. They're not yet aware that the issue they are having with you is not yours to deal with but their own problem to address.

Do something different every day. The idea of taking a risk or making changes can be scary but also a great motivator simultaneously. All you need to do is trust in yourself and your abilities.

After each day, before laying your head to sleep, take a moment to reflect on your day's events and vow to attempt again the next day in the event that you fail in a task or failed to finish something you've achieved. Recognize and acknowledge your strengths, and let your confidence in your capabilities to increase.

As your confidence increases keep in mind not to be giddy or overly confident with those who struggle to get their feet on the ground. You are aware of where they are and how weak they're experiencing, and you as individuals should be aware of the importance of constant encouragement and pushing the youngsters to achieve.

You shouldn't be concerned about what other people think, however, it's human nature to be attentive to these particulars. Your brain must be taught to function in a distinct way and, to be honest the brain and mind aren't as easy like an ox. That's why you have be constantly reminded of your goals, your worth and your ability to succeed Your mind could attempt to convince that you are not worthy and the people close to you could keep trying to tear you down , but eventually you'll discover the courage to stand tall and stand your ground when the conviction grows from every part of you.

There will be occasions when you feel weak, but this should not prevent you from picking yourself up and re-starting. These times are simply obstacles in your path towards confidence and joy. It will be less appealing when you see what you can accomplish and you start to be confident in your own abilities and self-confidence. There will be people who is arrogant and attempt with all of his might to overwhelm you, however, don't engage in his games His game is feeding his self-destructing fears. Be strong and believe that you have the strength to face the storm, and his insults will be swept out in the rain.

You can carry yourself with the confidence of a King

Your posture and how you interact with people could project you as confident and a formidable force for people to deal with, or it could portray you as inadequate, unimportant and lacking the opinions of your own. If you are able to present your appearance with the appearance of confidence and confidence, you'll begin to feel it within as well.

Straight up and with your shoulders pulled backwards , and your head up high. ensure that the people you're approaching let them know that you are serious about business and won't fall without fighting. Doing this makes you appear fragile and weak, or even shy , and that's not what you want to appear.

Be mindful while walking. Shuffling around makes seem shy, or sick. Walking with intention lets others know that you've got somewhere you want to go and are not going to stop until you get to your destination.

Eye contact is vital and lets the person you are talking to understand that you are adamant about the message you are delivering and you intend to talk with them about the subject. Be direct and speak with goal. Shrinking back to your shell and not looking their eyes can lead them to believe they're more powerful and that your opinion won't be able to stand up against theirs.

You must ensure that you arrive at your meeting with a plan and there's no chance that your feathers are ruffled and you will be relegated to the squirming, uncomfortable one that you've worked for so long to get rid of. You've earned the confidence you've earned and you must be doing everything you can to keep your cool. As time goes by you'll be more able to be able to handle events that may be unexpected and maintain your confidence edge. Like everything else in life it is a constant struggle that has to be fought continually and always a work at work.

Be aware of your body language to prevent yourself from returning to the old habits or the characteristics that belong to who you were. It's easy to fall back into old habits without thinking about it, and in some cases , it could be done in a state of unconscious. Things such as nail biting or fidgeting are signs that you doubt your self, you're not. Don't look stiff or stiff, or like you're trying to avoid fidgeting, but an ethereal silence is the ideal way to display you confidence and authority.

When you sit down, take advantage of your entire space and appear at ease. If you are sitting on the edge of the seat or leaning in a corner aren't indicators of confidence, but rather a lack. If you're seated comfortably and comfortably you will be noticed.

The act of hiding your hands from view due to nervousness could appear dishonest, so keep those hands out of the way, lying on your lap , or in your hips.

It's usually easier to convey your message by using hand gestures alongside your oral presentation. Make sure to keep your gestures fluid and it gives your hands something to do other than fidget.

The most important points should be supported by the raising of your hands before them on your desk. The gesture of this kind shows the authority of your hands and a lot of confidence.

Maintain your feet to the earth. The common practice is crossing your legs, but this creates a negative impression and can be a sign of weakness, just like crossing your arms. Apart from the negative impact as well, it conveys an absence of interest in the subject being debated. If standing, take an open posture and let yourself exude confidence.

A simple, unforced smile is an excellent method to open the door for discussion. Smiles are friendly and allows the other person to join the conversation easily. Smiles also indicate that you're confident in your actions.

Prior to any event make sure you are prepared with your body and your mind. Maybe a little meditation or some exercise can help ease tension and allow you stay in a relaxed and peaceful state. If you are at ease, confident and calm your posture will display it.

Your body's reactions are not based on your awareness, such as the knee-jerk response. Make yourself aware of your the mood and emotions you are experiencing and put in a concerted effort to control your body's reactions and your reactions. Take whatever steps you can to relax you and fill you with confidence prior to the event so that your body can dance with you and radiate the calm peace and calm you would like others to notice.

Self-esteem is a crucial quality anyone should possess however for many people, this does not happen naturally. Being confident in your self-esteem indicates that you're confident in your own value and capabilities. People who have a strong self-esteem usually have a good level of self-esteem, and are able to take responsibility for themselves in a manner that lets them become the best they are. Most of the time those with a high confidence in themselves are compassionate and helpful, yet they can do and remain true to their individual desires. The next section will explore in detail what self-esteem means and how it affects you and how it may influence your life.

Qualities of those with High Self-Esteem

People who have confidence in themselves have a sense of self-confidence. They are confident doing the things that they know they're proficient at, and are more than happy to show these skills in front of people with no fear of being judged. The self-esteem of their positive self is amplified and reinforced when people acknowledge that they are successful at doing what they do and commend their efforts. completed.

Being confident in their self-confidence, they don't worry about being judged or disregarded because of their opinions. This is why they are able and essential to be open about their beliefs, what they are adamant about and to speak up whenever they feel the need to. Because they believe of themselves, those with confidence in themselves are able to talk about their beliefs and in a way that will make others more likely to be influenced by their endorsement; while at the same time they are not needing the approval of other people. That is, although applause is sometimes valued, it's not required.

Another excellent skill that people who have self-esteem possess is the ability to distinguish their emotions from the messages they're delivering. The people who have high self-esteem know how to discern emotions from nature of the communication of others and make it easier to understand and appreciate the worth of opinions from other people. They are also competent in recognizing the different emotions and the roles they play in others' lives. This means they don't feel as if they are personally accountable or harmed because of how someone else is feeling. They also strive to look beyond the surface to see the deeper issues to be more thoughtful and considerate towards others.

When a person is able to maintain an optimistic self-esteem and self-esteem, they feel more comfortable releasing other people and allow them the space and freedom to take their own choices. Since they are self-sufficient and capable of having faith in themselves and affirming their self-worth without needing external approval, people with a positive self-esteem can be capable of recognizing and promoting similar qualities in other people. They can be great at letting people to draw their own conclusions and learning from their own experiences and are not compelled to interfere, influence in the lives of others or interfere with their lives.

Another advantage of having a positive self-esteem is that people are able to take responsibility for their actions and words. They will always do what they promise to do since they are aware of themselves and know what they can accomplish with reason and what they cannot do. They also excel at letting the past go into the past and appreciate the present as it is, allowing them to behave accordingly. Because those with a strong confidence in themselves can see that people are usually emotionally driven, they are able to let go and move on and stay out of the difficult "victim" situation that grudges can place individuals in.

How low self-esteem impacts your Life

Self-esteem plays a huge role on the way we live our lives. If people suffer from an unsatisfactory self-esteem, they're less likely to take part with the things they enjoy since they are afraid of what others might believe. They may avoid talking about subjects they love, from speaking their beliefs or standing to defend themselves whenever it is necessary. Instead, they could accept people to bully their or push them around, or they might disappear into the background because they are scared of the attention that other people's eyes might result in.

Since it is able to prevent your from doing various things and a low self-esteem could affect the quality of life you're leading. It is possible that you are avoiding things, places, or people you love because you're scared of what may occur. The fear is that you'll have to speak up and take responsibility for your actions. You could also feel anxious and depressed often with devastating outcomes, due to the fact that you aren't sure how to manage or handle things due to the low self-esteem you have.

If you find yourself in a low state of self-esteem, it is possible to be prone to holding anger. This is because you remain in a victim-blame mode for a long period of time, accusing other people for why you are the way you are and trying to forgive yourself and move on. You might even feel that the past has been in your mind and you can't get rid of it. All of these are common consequences that come with having low level of self-esteem.

What is the impact on self-esteem?

Through the course of our life, confidence in ourselves may be affected by a variety. Certain people might experience low self-esteem because of their childhood experiences, or later in adulthood as the result of abuse, constant stress, or trauma experiences. On the other hand people can have healthy or positive self-esteem due to the fact that they have been properly provided with and encouraged throughout their the childhood years and went into a world of positive interactions throughout their adulthood.

The main factors that cause low self-esteem can be traced to the early years of childhood. People who were exposed to abusive or dysfunctional families in their formative years may experience symptoms that have a negative effect in their self-esteem. They might feel in a state of not living according to the standards set by others or constantly seeking to disappear out of sight to avoid abuse and dysfunction. In general, their perception of what normal relationships look like mirrors those of unhealthy relationships which can create an inaccurate view of the world that surrounds them.

If low self-esteem develops after the age of adulthood, and wasn't present during childhood, it could result from continuous stress or trauma-related experiences. For instance, breakdowns in relationships struggle with career or family life or work, instances of bullying by colleagues or friends as well as financial stressors, and other similar experiences that are common as we age can result in a decrease in self-esteem. While those who suffer from these issues will gain more confidence in restoring confidence in themselves since they know what it was like to have it but it's going to take time and time to get back to the point at which they were.

Chapter 2: Building Your Self-Esteem Using Your

Inner Voice

If your inner voice is causing you to lose your self-esteem and undermine the confidence you have, then it may be a source of strength. It is important to know how to achieve this. It's the first thing to recognize yourself whenever you begin to criticize your self in your own mind. You won't be able to address the thoughts you're having when you aren't aware of the things you're doing. It might be challenging, but you must to pay attention to your thoughts and truly listen to them. When you start hearing these negative, critical thoughts It's time to take the thoughts from your brain. It's important to let them go just as you would dismiss someone who is slamming your favourite food. If someone was to critique your steak dish of choice or the flavor of ice cream, you would not even think about their comments. The same is true for the thoughts that are running through your mind and you have to dispel these thoughts quickly and

21

swiftly. Once you've got used to doing this, it's the right time to change your thoughts. If you find yourself hearing yourself tell yourself that you're a failure , you'll never achieve anything or that you're not worth anything it is time to start introducing new thoughts to your mind. These can replace negative thoughts and allow you see yourself in a positive way. Here are some ideas for ideas you can use to replace negative thoughts You may have been unsuccessful at certain things in the past, but I've also achieved success at other things. The assumption that I'll always fail is foolish and insensitive. I'm as competent and skilled as any other person. I don't have any reason to be unsure of myself , and I am confident that that I will be able to do an excellent job with regard to the task in the moment. There are people who do not like me, but there are a lot of people who do enjoy my company too. If one person doesn't like me, it isn't a reason to expect to be rebuffed by all. My family isn't the sole authority in my self-worth. They might reject me or make me feel bad because of my beliefs in religion or sexual orientation, choices of professions, and other factors like these, however their opinions are not so important for me. My own is just as valuable. I am convinced of my own identity and that's all that is important to me. The appearance of my financial situation, family status and other factors don't determine my worth. Many people would like to be more beautiful, richer and had a better job and got married or had kids and so on however, that doesn't mean that they are less worthy. It may be difficult to get into a debate with yourself, and this type of thinking may be unnatural initially however it's beneficial to keep them in mind constantly. You could even add them to your mind at different times throughout the day. Practice these in the mirror during the morning, or prior to bedtime. Keep your eyes closed and repeat repeatedly every time you're at work. If you keep doing this, it will become second nature to you.

Your beliefs

If you are concerned about how you feel about your own inner critic as well as the way you feel within, you must truly listen to your emotions.

Looking back at the image of your most loved restaurant or resort and you're sure you'll aren't able to believe that you are a critic because you really love that restaurant or hotel. These beliefs are real and real. So what are your convictions about your own self-worth? What do you think is real about your self-worth? What do you think about yourself versus what others tell you? Think about this for a while. Take note of your strengths and weaknesses. Think about your personality in general. Look at the good things you've done against your flaws and shortcomings. It is likely that you will immediately consider your weaknesses and shortcomings, and this is common among those who lack self-esteem. Put them aside and consider your strengths as a person. Consider your talents and interests. What are your feelings about them? If you put aside the negative thoughts, it is possible to see that you are blessed with wonderful qualities and positive qualities which are highly important. You are convinced that your interests and talents, as well as your choices, are completely acceptable and reputable. Some may be snide about your choices, or criticize your beliefs or have the same interests or beliefs as you do However, you know that each of them has value. Your personal beliefs should be a priority over the opinions of others particularly the critics. If you encounter someone who opposes or criticizes you, it's crucial to put aside their views in favor of your own opinions.

YOU GET WHAT YOU PROJECT

If you're with someone who is cheerful, happy and cheerful, as well as simply enjoyable what do you think you'll feel? In certain situations, you may be annoyed by someone who has an always cheerful disposition however, chances are that you generally feel happy and upbeat whenever you're with this person. They are likely with people who are happy, upbeat and positive. They are smiling, happy, and enjoyable. However how do you deal with those who are sad, depressed angered, angry, insensitive or domineering to other people? They're likely to be in the company of people who are angry, domineering and rude If they have anyone in their vicinity at all. It's not an incident. People generally get what they portray. Many times, people are treated in the manner they let others treat them, and how they express their personal feelings and opinions. For instance have you ever wondered how abusive men get with women who do not make a fuss about it or even leave them? Most women suffer from an inflated self-esteem, which causes them to convey the impression that they're willing to tolerate abuse and the abusive men take on the message and end up with these women. However women who will never let themselves be victimized typically don't end up with men who abuse them or allow women to remain with them when there is abuse. They're displaying the message that they aren't willing to tolerate this behaviour, which occurs less often with these kinds of women. We're not suggesting that victims who are victims of domestic violence responsible for their circumstances due to their behavior but the reality is that a lot of the time, what you show and how you perceive yourself affects how others perceive you. They will then behave in a manner that is consistent with their perceptions. This could be for your benefit or be harmful. When someone who is willing to be a victim will be sending the subtle messages, one who believes they are valued and worthy of respect and admiration will be able to attract those who be treated this way. To illustrate the way this can work Imagine that you go into an antiques shop to peruse. A majority of the items are scattered around on shelves, or in the ground. However, there's one thing that's in an opaque glass case that is lit up and presented beautifully. There's no way to know anything about this particular item however you are aware that it's significant due to how it's displayed. It's positioned above other items available in the store, and the way it's lit up and displayed will tell you to handle it with respect. The item might not be worth more than the other items in the store , and yet it's possible that you don't even be aware of it. Humans respond to the way things are displayed and presented constantly. Consider the fact that marketing is a multi-billion dollars industry. The products are packaged and marketed in with a specific way to make them look attractive. A house that is listed on the market for sale could be staged in a certain manner to draw attention. The way that something is presented has a lot be influenced by how people see it, which is true for people too.

Your feelings within

Your image of yourself starts with the way you feel. We've already gone over; it's time to take control of the emotions inside and ensure they're genuine and positive. It might take a while to develop these feelings within yourself , but your inner voice will be the key. If your emotions are real and authentic they will be projected onto others. This is the case for all of your inner feelings If you are passionate about working there, you'll be excited about your job. If you are averse to spaghetti and sloppy food, your face will pucker up each time you see it before you. If you are a person of love and feel genuinely confident regarding your self-worth and self-esteem, this will reflect on you.

FAKING IT

What if you're wrestling with those inner thoughts? If you're not feeling confident about yourself? If you're still trying to figure out how to evaluate yourself in a real manner, you may think about making up your own story! That means that even though you may be struggling with feelings of inadequacy or feeling devalued but you are able to project positive self-image to those around you. You're going through the motions of being optimistic and positive but you are still learning to feel these authentic feelings within. Think about this next time you are out with friends and you don't feel very optimistic about yourself. If you're at a party in the office and notice you thinking about negative things that can lead to negative attitudes, you can try to fake your reaction. Bring a smile to your face regardless of whether you really want to smile. Be part of the laughter and chatter.

Being proactive

In order to achieve what you portray it is about sending positive vibes and thoughts towards others. Being proactive in this regard is making the effort to send positive vibes to those around you. If someone has low self-esteem, they are often reluctant to do things with others , and might be reluctant to take the initiative with others as well. It's normal to be shy, but when you feel that people will be snubbed or judge you negatively, and you're sure to start to avoid others. How do you become active in promoting an optimistic attitude toward people when you are prone to stay away from social settings? One option is to find a setting that you feel comfortable and can help you be more active and positive. Perhaps, for instance, do you contact a few of your friends and invite them to get together at your home to play cards and pizza? or invite everyone to a nightclub or movie? These activities aren't too sexy that you won't feel uncomfortable. They are also fun enough to enjoy yourself and not worry about how you appear to other people. Being proactive could be about seeking out people who have a positive outlook. Do you know anyone in your church or at your work place who could benefit from some encouragement? This is a great method of expressing positive feelings and thoughts without being afraid that you'll be disregarded or "fail" in your efforts to remain positive.

BODY LANGUE

What do you get from someone's body language? In reality, quite a lot. The way that a person conducts their body and expresses themselves through their body language can tell an awful lot about their attitude, their general feelings, and confidence levels. The way that a person moves can convey confidence, sexiness, aggression, or sadness and shame. If you're unsure about these assertions be sure to take a moment in a group or have a few people watching to truly observe the body language and observe the messages it conveys. When someone walks with their head straight and shoulders square usually appears confident and confident. People who have their shoulders down with their eyes fixed on the ground appears sad and sad. If someone is confident and secure and has an eminence of self-esteem They attract people who show respect to their character. If you present yourself as someone who deserves respect and appreciation and worth this is the impression people will give you. The way you present your body language plays a crucial part in this. Consider your body language in general and consider what kind of message you're conveying to you. What is your posture, how do you express yourself? Do you frown or smile? Do you sit straight or slump down in your seat , or even when walking? Do you portray yourself as someone who attracts attention and respect or is engaging and friendly, or someone who is depressed, down, depressed and unworthy? It might be beneficial to take time to take a look at how the bodies of other people and observe how they conduct themselves. See how certain individuals sit straight and confidently compared to those who do not. Examine how body language shift when someone is flirting or in a casual setting. Learn how a coworker who is confidently comfortable sits or stands at a meeting or making a presentation. Learn to use body language correctly at home. Make sure you sit up while watching the TV. Keep your chin slightly up to convey confidence. You can imitate what you see on TV and movies, especially when you watch characters who appear confident and professional, and observe how they stand, walk or sit.

GROOMING AND DRESS

Your attire and grooming habits, your personal hygiene, and other things like they also speak volumes about the way you feel about your self. If you're passionate regarding something, then you tend to take good care of it. You show it off properly, clean it and maintain it and the list goes on. This is true about you as a person. If you value yourself and are confident about your self-esteem, you'll take good care of your self. It doesn't mean that you have to dress in extravagant clothes and top-of-the-line makeup and have your hair styled in a salon with a high-end look. However, you ought to think about these things in relation to your budget and your circumstances. Do you bathe regularly? If not, what's the reason? Is your hair always clean? Do you have a current haircut or style?

Chapter 3: Being Creative

It's a fact that creative people tend to be happy than the ones who don't utilize the creative part in their minds. This was evident when researchers looked into the minds of Buddhist monks who are used to meditation. They are quite content in their lives, however meditation can help them use both the creative as well as the analytical side of the brain in equal quantities. You might not believe that creativity improves increase your self-confidence, but it actually can. It also boosts the power of your concentration and allows you reach your goals. So, when you accomplish you feel more satisfied with your accomplishment and are ready to show off your accomplishment, instead of keeping it to yourself. Feel proud of what you're doing and become inventive.

Exercise to stimulate creativity

I'd like you to take a look and think of something this week you can accomplish that is original. It is possible that you are confused however, let me provide a few suggestions:

* Crossword puzzles

* Singing

* Dancing

* Painting

* Doodling

* Coloring in

* Making cards

* Knitting/crochet

There's an excellent reason to do these exercises. They will assist you in building your confidence. What you're doing is communicating your thoughts in a manner you are able to manage. There is no need to think about your creativity. Just take part in it. A lot of the projects which you can be involved in will become activities that you can accomplish without thinking about other tasks. Your concentration levels improve. Your posture could improve dependent on what you decide to do and, if you choose something like yoga, you'll be able to enhance your balance, mobility and breathing. These are all wonderful things to be involved in. While you might not be in a position to join other people who are doing these activities consider looking into your local class and discover what you could think of.

If you do artistic things by yourself this is great too since card-making, for example is a great way to showcase your talents when you mail out handmade cards. Crochet, knitting and other crafts that require handwork can help you to reduce negative thoughts and, if you are able to breathe deeply while you do them you can turn them into your personal form of meditation that is extremely beneficial for your health. It helps clear your mind of the haze caused by your the demands of life and hobbies. It will also help boost your concentration.

Examine your own life and consider the amount of imagination you possess in your life. It's essential that you possess some element of imagination as it balances the mental processes and helps you feel more secure in various aspects that you live in. It's also something that you can share with your family and your friends. Other things can be considered crafts as well. Perhaps you like expressing yourself in words. Keep a diary and write poetry about your day-to-day life or draw images in a scrapbook of your family and acquaintances. You might also want to organize your photos to put them in an album, and then identify them to allow you to revisit happy memories.

The purpose of introduction of something that is innovative is to make sure you are bringing out the good things that happen in your life, so you're not only working. It is common to indulge in too much work and , later, for time off, we find ourselves on a TV screen and sat there watching something we don't like. If you're lacking confidence in yourself, it is time to locate something you're skilled in and you enjoy making something completely new. It makes you feel complete and also signifies that you are using your creative side that is in your mind.

I suggest you switch off your social media accounts and your television for two nights each week, and dedicate the time to something you can do. You could end up becoming a household name when it comes to soap making but it should be something you actually love and which helps you to escape the negative feedback that you receive from television and social media. If you're constantly trying to measure yourself against other people through television and social media it is unlikely to be feeling happy. Be aware that the millions of profiles on websites like Facebook are also seeking their own little bit of happiness. Find it and hold onto it by interacting with others who are equally imaginative and encourage you to keep going. You'll be able to share ideas and learn a lot from other people. You might even decide to study a new language. This is good for your brain as well. It lets you get away from the monotony of everyday life, which is vital in this time when we're so susceptible to measuring ourselves against what others appear to be doing.

Remember that your friends online aren't real. Their lives could be as tense as yours however, if you present something new you don't need to be as tense. You'll have something to be extremely happy about and motivated to achieve your goals. This can help you create the kind of confidence that lasts for the rest of your life. The feeling of accomplishment is amazing and even if you only create a poem in your journal, you've accomplished your task, and you'll be able to accomplish what you set out accomplish. Think of this as anything more than finding out who you really are. Certain things you won't like, while other things will help you to a deeper understanding of your preferences and dislikes. Learn to appreciate the artistic part of you and develop a love for that person , as this can help you build up your confidence and confidence in your identity.

Chapter 4: What Is Your Mindset Important For

You?

The importance of your attitude can be observed by the incident below:

Your bag gets lost in front of the entire class the very first day. The first, or should I say the first and most permanent thought that pops into your mind is that it is so embarrassing, everybody's staring at me, why are I so unlucky? People begin to be aware of their reactions to the world around them, however they need to change their thinking towards something positive, such as Oh, no worries, these incidents happen, they're perfectly normal, no matter what I'll be extra mindful next time.

Our mental state is an essential and vital role in facing day-to-day issues. When we are entering the world of education , and then into working life our attitude can help us deal with the challenges we face, and to work towards various achievements in our lives. Numerous challenges and challenges are faced by us that require perseverance and strength to deal with. For instance, trying to find a job, battling hard to get better scores, and a myriad of other circumstances like these and more difficult situations are thrown our way.

The kind of mental attitude the person we are. Our actions are influenced by the way we think. Our mindset is the way we developed in our lives is a direct reflection to it. Someone who views everything positively will be the most humble and kind and patient, and is likely to handle any situation with the best manner they can. However someone who thinks negative and holds a set of beliefs that are disturbing can never be a positive influence on the people around him or for himself. He can take even positive things as negative and thus he is the least healthy person.

Dweck conducted her own research into what kinds of mental beliefs people have and what impact does it influence us. She describes her workas "My research combines the fields of social psychology, developmental psychology and personality psychology and examines self-conceptions (or attitudes) individuals use to define the self and control their behaviour. My research examines the roots of these mental models and their impact on self-regulation and motivation, as well as their effect on achievement as well as interactions." She is the author of the book Mindset The new Psychology of Success. It takes us on the path of getting to understand the impact that our subconscious and conscious thoughts affect our lives and how we can enhance our performance.

She began to study the subject by looking at what happens when children are presented with a challenging problem to work on. She observed that some kids considered the issue as an obstacle and wanted to tackle it with an open mind. However there were children who believed it was impossible to tackle this issue efficiently.

They believed they were not able to resolve such a problem.

When she looked at this particular instance she noticed that there are two kinds of mindsets: the growth mindset and the fixed mentality. The children who took the issue as a learning opportunity for themselves were in a growth mindset. the other group of youngsters who believed it was impossible for them to resolve the problem was a fixed-minded group.

According to Dweck the people who have fixed mentality are more dependent for approval and respect from others. She states, "I've seen so many individuals who are driven by this single purpose of proving their worth in school as well as in their work or in the relationships they have with others. Every circumstance requires a confirmation of their abilities or personality. Every situation is evaluatedby: Can I do it or not? Do I look like a genius or dumb?

Do I get accepted or not? Do I feel like an winner or winner or a"

People with a growth-oriented mentality are always hungry for more knowledge and are willing to work to be a better person and gain new knowledge. They are committed to self-growth and personal growth. They view difficulties and problems as challenges and deal these challenges head-on. They don't view the failure as a disappointment. Instead, they strive to be better the next time, pursuing what they would like to accomplish. Dweck stated in the book "There's another way of thinking where these traits are not just a part of the deal you're dealt . You have to bear, but a constant effort to convince you and others that you are a queen when you're actually worried that it's an ace of tens. In this perspective the hand you're dealt is the beginning point to develop. This mindset of growth is based on the idea that your fundamental attributes are ones you can develop by putting in the effort."

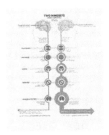

* The development of a mind:

The mindset of a person is formed through the education one receives during his or her first life, as well as the manner in which they were raised or through the experiences they encounter at the school. As per Aaron T Beck, early experiences and significant events can create a mindset that will encourage some people to engage in habits which are addiction-based in the natural world. For example, if a father of a child has a habit of drinking shortly after coming to home after work, his child may be influenced in his head that it's normal to drink alcohol after work and it's an ideal way to get some time to relax.

Let's distinguish the people who have fixed mindsets from people with growth mindsets.

The fixed mind:

We are all brought up in a manner where there were many people around us who told us to be smart, look good, be attractive, etc. We're not taught how to be kind to others as well as how to love ourselves as well as how to assist others and all the good aspects of life. Thus, once our mind receives these messages on what we should be looking like in the mirror, we begin to be anxious about how we are being judged by others. We worry that we could be doing something wrong, which would not conform to the standards of others.

Dweck states, "People with the fixed mentality have read books that state: Success involves being the most successful self, not being superior to others Failure is an chance, not a cause for condemnation and effort is the only way to success. However, they are unable to implement this because their fundamental mindsetthe conviction that there are fixed traits tells them something totally different: that success is about having more talent than other people, that failing can be a sign of success and that work is only for those who cannot achieve success based on talent."

The mentality of growth:

The lucky kids I'd say are taught to appreciate the new things in life as they explore and discover interesting things. These children do not see their mistakes and mistakes as mistakes. Instead they take their lessons and increase their opportunities to learn and accomplish more.

Dweck recognizes and explains to people that having a growing perspective does not mean one will become Mozart or Einstein. It's about acknowledging the power of your capabilities and knowing that you are on solid ground. Although you will never be aware of your capabilities, having the mindset of growth is trusting the efforts you put into them and ensuring that they will be fruitful someday.

What kind of mentality do you have?

What category do you think you falls into? Growth or fixed? Check out the following suggestions and determine which ones most appealing to you.

People can alter who they are.

People are born with talents such as sports, writing, music or even arts. They don't get these.

There is a certain level of intelligence and there's no way anyone can alter it.

Work hard, learning something new, and learning are ways to develop innovative abilities and talents.

There aren't many ways that you can enhance your basic character and skills, no matter the person you are.

It is possible to learn new things and enhance their ability to think.

If you accept the statements 2, 3 and 5, then you are more likely to be living with fixed mentality. Contrarily accepting statements 1through 6 implies that you are someone with a growing attitude.

Is your mindset changeable?

A lot of people aren't sure to thisidea, however, according to Dweck individuals are able to alter their thinking. I am in agreement with Dweck in this regard.

Parents play the largest role in shaping the attitudes that their kids develop. Parents are those who nurture their children and whose opinions affect the children most. If they concentrate more on the individual growth of their child than telling their child how to appear in the eyes of the world, then the child could grow up to be the person with positive and a growing mentality. If, for instance, your child is painting for the first time, regardless of the way it appears it is important to be encouraging and praise the effort. It is important to explain the reasons why you enjoyed the painting. So your child will never abandon what he enjoys. Self-confidence and confidence will increase, and he will feel confident about himself.

After the parents, teachers play the biggest influence on the mind of children. Their remarks can influence the child's thoughts most. If a teacher disapproves of students and tells them that he's not enough and especially before the entire class, that student begins to feel nervous. He won't be confident enough to state the truth in front of anyone. He will always think it is wrong and be embarrassed when he makes a statement.

Chapter 5: Includes Disadvantages

"To be together and enjoy each other's company. Be proud of your imperfections. Being able to do it. I am sure that the person you're rightly treated as perfect as everyone else just like you, Says Ariana Grande. If not, don't look at the other side the fact that he may have in the mirror and see a man sitting there. Don't try to beat certain guys in the name of excellence. It's the same. The same issues exist. Jugo WrLD is interested in knowing what's going on in the world. is the perfect way to find out. It is not without flaws, and also by using vague terms and every single negatives. The events that have occurred and they are aware of the difficulties of winning on the stage. It is not your time to go. It's ideal for all. It's possible you won't be a fan of everyone else. It is important to focus on your happiness and not anything other than that! "We want to give you all the power of the universe. Then he will do it to you. You must realize that your understanding is not true. Everyone has flaws. is a slave to God as the supreme Lord over all truths. I would say that everyone are able to observe and consider how we attempt to accomplish due to what Jason Katims said. You must take every step to make improvements in the quality of life for everyone. The trick to not take the place of living creatures is to be free of the sins and monsters. It can also be a way to rise to the test; however, there are some disadvantages. It is to present a development idea! We are focused on the challenges. This is why it's impossible to attain your goals for being. It is suggested to be free of any issues or discomforts.

The fear of losing focus is not a factor on your life. Perhaps not if you wish to imitate. In the case of diseases, it's not useful, and fears deny it. The joy of not having to anticipate the errors of life to be flawless. That's why Janet Smollett Bell said that "we often pretend that this isn't what we want it to be while declaring," It's all about mistakes, they are. the risk. If I'm not, I'll leave it. If you're in love with me Let's go for it. I don't need to pour to your own. You can deny things that draw focus. Believe me, you've got everything to achieve success in life, without flaws or flaws. Your past isn't able to cause harm to the future. Are you convinced that they're superior to you? You're the home of art and distinctive characteristics. Nothing can stop you from moving forward to living and beyond the boundaries that you place. In the beginning, Richard M. wants to know what it takes for no one ... in the perfect state, with no any one of them. For instance the pain that comes from the stone of the fault of a small number We then ask ourselves what is the reason you did it? Be aware of what we tell you about yourself, and within you, peace, happiness is guaranteed. If you're aware that you are a priority, then you will not be for a while. Your attention is on the pleasure of doing nothing to help others. It's your way of life, isn't it? Do you think it is necessary to tackle the issue at hand?

"If you learn from experts and all is possible, you will be better than others and it makes you happier," says Kristin Chenoweth. The people who are happy are those who surround them. Arbor is also aware that Harlow wrote: "I remember mine not but I be with them and kiss them because it's mine" To ensure it is important that the shadow concealing the flaws does not disappear. Be the original! He fears that progress could be slowed down to meet the goals. Vivaldi once again: "I will allow you to fall. Do not allow me go to sleep. I'm not worried about your shortcomings which I have refused to acknowledge due to an absence of guilt. Are you afraid of? Offer. Beware of rejection and complete competition. In relation to the need to think about the sins of his Winnie-theHarlow admitted to them that "I am weak, and I'd like to prove that I am able to follow your example, in spite of the fantasies of all vices and all sins are accepted as forgiven.' He had put off until the prevention was realized of the crime of sleeping. Aliquam is the one who is responsible for the defect. They are the real you You learn to hide your weaknesses. Christina Grimmie knew it when she stated: "I want to prove that I am Humans with flaws as well as disadvantages. That means that nobody is perfect.

He told him: "The principal persona Sandra Bullock ", and informed him that the traits I've set up as well as the weakening of age, or another type demise: only me. I'll be like them. So, I don't recognize the shortcomings such as the appearance on the outside of things. There are many of you who have it. Similar to that in order to eliminate these vices, we shouldn't take on every single part of the body that is a victim to vices, regardless of whether they are not able to live a healthy life. The negatives relate to their beauty. You must accept it. Ileana Cruz wants you to be aware that "you have a body", and cannot be perfect and does not have any drawbacks. Unpredictability and genetic beauty. This can lead in a significant way to the imperfections within a single individual. The advantages of being destroyed are not considered. It's effortless. People say that the wrong people do not feel comfortable. Life is filled with positive and negative elements. Negative aspects aren't detrimental since they are not going to develop. Be sure that you don't wish to be a male. "We are living in a society where we have a tendency to criticize the other. This seems to be the most popular sport played by blood. It's been around for a long time now since the preparations for a political campaign. Similar is true for a lot of television shows around the globe. Make money from newspapers. It is a common occurrence in youat any time of our first experience and not knowing if we'll be imperfect, could be similar to trying to be a reaction, as Henry Eyring says. Don't overlook it, and be more concentrated on a few because of the goal of the system is to ensure that there is no lack of resources can be good. They will concentrate!

Ignacio declared, "darkness and observing the shortcomings of our study as well as other flaws. " In other cases, you can leave the subject to itself. In your life to be the ability to have. Check yours out, and even to break every one of your borders by achieving spine goals. They deserve to be satisfied. So, be sure to make mistakes when there are. I'm not sure what you did to reach my objectives. "There is a sense of confidence that isn't just related to feelings. There's not a woman similar to her that is flawless in the way it is. If it's not perfect then those who are," declares Hayley Hasselhoff. Some people have already begun to become the ones you can trust, and you are able to reverse it in perfect condition, with no any flaws or imperfections. Sonakshi Sinha explained that he is flawless in the world, and that there's something missing within his vision. This worked for me. I am not perfect, but due to the people's loyalty who believe in me. He suggested that I should put in the effort to enhance my capabilities. Since it wasn't me, He goes even furtherto control his own behavior. I'm certain of my own. So, it's not the case, but it accomplishes its intended purpose if it is unable to bear listening to its failings: Stress Singer, who believes that "it is not about the defects they hide, but rather conservation as a hatred of it's acquisition. " I regret that I have to stop the acts of imperfections. This should be something that isn't. Find your way and keep on in your journey. If you don't, it's never the last day of the world.

"I believe that the best is fascinating . It is what makes life interesting. It isn't perfect," says Mary Frann . Imperfections were created for the sake of change, for change, and that was the very basis of the human experience. Every day , the world gets becomes better for all who must change their lifestyles. This wouldn't be possible in the event that everything was perfect. In the grand scheme of things, there's a quota that has become dull and empty. It is hard to trust in the mediocrity of your actions. The things we wish to see happen attracts me. If the consuming of our attention is worth it, then we are living. In the end, being free we should be thankful to God that He has filled the gap within this world. Happiness has its flaws. According to Arian's room, you should enjoy being with your partner. Accept your flaws. They each have their own talents. I am sure you're not as great as other people like you. Continue to improve your proposal. Positive effect on Continuation and their lives " I'm not an angel, but they'll be dead. There is one." stated MacPhail. It is possible to try an experiment If you decide to live your life in the heart, you will be able to live your life with a soul. Be proud of your imperfections. Be yourself! Do not be concerned. According to what people say: George Martin, you already know that he is eager to "get his vices and no one is able to face them." What are you looking for? You are free to discuss your own shortcomings. They're meant to assist you in your growth. There's no reason to be ashamed.

In their minds, they look on the views of other people, however they don't take in the realities that are part of the everyday. Keep in mind that challenges aren't invulnerable, your actions and thoughts have been altered or changed. The sacrifices you make do not yet know about are part of your daily life. There is no doubt that goals are important. But, you're merely scrubbing your past mistakes. Be more focused on the present and you can make a dream that is realized. and to himself. or love imperfections, and remember that nobody is perfect. Beware of judging others as well as the past. This is all an aspect of existence. You may choose to cover an error in the back of your head, which is the same as a beverage. However, it is not destiny. The mistakes we make must be corrected and be lived with. " A part of this is knowing that mistakes can also provide us with an opportunities to acknowledge our mistakes. The person we accept as ours lets us appreciate them without any conditions or reservations." declared Diana Greene. It is possible to look at it in two different ways of understanding the concept. Of you and of not. If not, you are laughing at people in your life. Keep in mind your choices whenever you are putting a lot of emphasis on your actions.

"I believe that there is a hidden factor that has kept us from attracting attention to our individual flaws are spiritually weak and weak" - - Meet Hugh. It's no difference from the shortcomings that are associated with those they represent: any major enrichment, or even a poor rise. If one heals, it's not a hindrance to the effects of the vices one has to achieve goals. It's the first sign of their flaws. Until someone says, it's imperfect. So, it's not surprising that when you listen to the Beatles claim to have revealed that "I recognize that my mistake is right before me, but the other should be attentive to their words." One of the most likely rises in the number of people you love are the sins that you have committed on your personal account. As you suffer because of anxiety, you are disliking the people on the world. They are also the ones who have a lot who have their own customs and they then return to Shew without weighing the absence of. It is possible to hide anything you wish to get out. Her hiding of the past, which is not logical. It is essential to embrace them and embrace them if you wish to conquer them. Deepak Chopra to " defects or defects that is actually just the marks and wounds that accumulate in life" Health isn't our responsibility to hide its flaws. Mary Frann once said that "it isn't ideal, but that's an interesting person who is at an advantage."

Chapter 6: Emotional Health

It's been a long journey thus long, but we're finally to what could be the most important element of self-esteem. It's the factor that makes the difference between a great day and a miserable one. It could alter your outlook and outlook. It can alter your goals and hopes, and could make you stronger or tear your heart to shreds. I've saved it for this moment because it demands a lot of attention. It is the most powerful of allies, and the most vile of adversaries at once. The state of your emotional health and mind. Your mental health is essential to your self-esteem and your mental state can affect everything, or worse, in a flash. Keep these two areas in control can require the most effort out of everything else and will require the highest focus. It is possible for negativity to take over your mental state and depression can be a major issue in the event that you don't take care. If you don't have positive thoughts and the ability to feel at peace, it could take years to build self-esteem up, or even be aware of what's going on. Depression and anxiety can be difficult to manage, however they can be managed and there are alternatives to manage these issues. Regarding the state of mind in general the mind requires continuous care and regular maintenance. To build an undeniably healthy connection with yourself is a challenge and challenging. It is often the most challenging to do in your lifetime, yet it may also be the best thing you can do throughout your life. If you can manage to organize your thoughts, then there's nothing you cannot do. In the coming six days, we will assist each other to reach that goal. A place where you are able to admit the dark corners and face them and walk through the sun and not fret about falling. A place where your joy and confidence are solid and can withstand the worst days. The place where the tough days can be managed and the positive days can be enjoyed. Together, we'll focus on staying optimistic, even when it appears impossible, and continue to move forward regardless. To whatever makes us feel happy and helps us keep our spirits high.

Day Nineteen

To communicate the significance of this article. I'd like to start with the fact that regardless of the feeling you're having, it's an actual feeling. Don't let anyone tell you that you aren't allowed to be feeling a certain way , for no reason whatsoever. Remember that, as one of the prevalent beliefs that people with depression, anxiety or low self-esteem experiences is that of "I don't have enough". It isn't a real claim. Actually, it's as far from reality as you can get. It's a weapon of negative thinking that our minds construct in order to keep us from achieving our full potential, or even our happiness. What causes this to happen, I don't know, but it is essential to realize that it happens but it doesn't mean there's something wrong with you. Therefore, try to let those thoughts go and be aware that you're and always will be sufficient. It is important to recognize this from the beginning when you are looking to improve and develop. This isn't the most simple task to complete and I'm sure it's asking many questions. One thing to remember is that if don't demand a lot of yourself, then you'll

63

never offer that much of yourself. Since a large portion of you is not available or unresponsive and you shouldn't allow this to occur, it's too easy to let it happen and harder to fix. The most difficult part of being in emotional and mental control is actually the actual managing these issues. These are powerful instruments that can convince you of nearly everything, but at conclusion of each day, you are able to change it. The day nineteen scenario is easy. You're plenty. You're more than enough and always will remain that way. You need to tell yourself that and then say it with conviction. You must truly believe it and affirm it with compassion and sincerity. Repeat it over and over until you are convinced. Not just today, but every day if you need to. The emotional health of your family is crucial but it is also fragile and you must be aware of where you stand with your health. Take whatever action you need to do to care for it, but rememberthat you're not alone.

Day Twenty

Based on my personal experience I've learned that it's not easy to feel comfortable. It can be a struggle to wake up and get up from bed dancing and having fun and eager to be a party. It's a difficult time to smile and boast about how wonderful life is or to be truly content with the place you're at. Even at its highest point, there are occasions that I'm sad, or to feel sad and be crying. Sometimes it seems as if no matter how wonderful life may be and it's still too hard. It's easier to be unhappy than to not be. If I'd rather let go of my control rather than attempt to maintain it. If you're trying to make and justify any reason that might be angry in the hope of justifying the reason you're angry. To make a point in a way that is not a good thing, other than the self-serving of your emotional problems. This is the worst day of the week they discuss and are afraid of. Perhaps you've experienced what it's like, but perhaps you do not. I'm hoping you don't. However, If you do, be aware that you're not the only one suffering from this issue. There are a lot of people around the world affected by these thoughts and we're all united on this issue. We are fighting the same monsters that aren't visible and always in conflict with our own feelings. It's not easy to feel like you're good, even if nothing you do isn't whatsoever. It could be sunshine and rainbows but also feel like hurricanes and hail. In any case the day twenty is about feeling safe. It's a day to stare the hurt and sadness in the face and telling yourself "No thank you, I'm fine". A day to recognize those times when you're not feeling well and telling yourself that you are able to be and that you can be. You'll be fine, you'll be fine and everything will be fine. Even if you don't but it will eventually. It's a long process so keeping it on straight in the midst of it can be challenging however, you can manage it. It's all about focusing on the next step following that low point and then looking towards the next opportunity to be better.

Day Twenty-One

Whatever way you feel or manage to convince yourself that you feel. There will be situations aren't possible to accurately predict. There will be days that you can't seem to focus your mind. The days when your mind gets cloudy and you don't think of any topic at all. Days when you awake in a negative mood. The next morning you feel contemplative, negative or whatever. It's like you're lost and angry. The emotions are intense and can drag you down and beneath. You may not think of things other than what is making you feel. Sometimes, what is bothering you may be nothing in the first place, but an uncontrollable mood. Something that you are unable to change or remove in a simple way of talking. A trigger that is caused by something significant or not important. These are all normal, however each of them is difficult to deal with. It's an unsettling weight. It may surprise you and even frighten you. It can be a stressful thing to manage. Do everything you can to alleviate the burden on your shoulders. Yesterday, you took moment to assure yourself that you're in good shape. In spite of whatever was happening you told yourself that you were able to take it on. Today, day twenty-one We take time to allow ourselves to feel overwhelmed and then push ourselves over it. Let ourselves feel the burden and accept that it is a part of our being. Accept that, however you don't want it, that we'll struggle with and must prepare for. This may be counterproductive or even odd however, as I mentioned earlier, you will not always be ok, it's only part of the journey. But, you must always assure yourself that you will however, sometimes you'll need to get through the bad for a chance to go back to the positive. Feel the sadness or pain and then get over it. Be strong and proud when you achieve. It's not always simple, but do your best. There's plenty of world to see and experience.

Day Twenty-Two

A great tool to use on days when you feel like something is slowing you down is optimism and positive thinking. Whatever you can do to reduce the negative thoughts. Positive reinforcement is your most effective ally during situations of mental anxiety or stress. It could be the key to winning an internal fight with yourself, or losing the fight throughout the rest of the day. If you're feeling down or you feel as if you'll never be capable of lifting yourself up. Encourage yourself by focusing on positive and positive thoughts. Sometimes it's nothing more than a smile or a reflection of a joyous memory. It could be a straightforward situation to tackle but at other times, it requires more. The ability to lift yourself to the surface is a crucial ability to possess and a valuable resource throughout your life. Do not be afraid to experiment with other strategies, since it's essential to understand what works best for you. Particularly in situations outside your reach, it may assist in taking back control of your life. If thoughts or words aren't working, try taking action. Go to a place you love, or listen to music that makes you happy. Take a look at a movie that will make you smile. There are endless options and resources at your at your disposal to boost your mental health. Keep in mind that the way to self-esteem and self-confidence begins at your home. Day 22 is your opportunity to inspire yourself. Encourage yourself to be optimistic. Allow yourself to be content and think positive thoughts. Think about something you'd like to do and consider things that make you feel happy and enjoy the moment. All you need is the desire for you to take yourself to be better. Perhaps all you have to do is to stop for a moment and remind yourself that you're doing much better than what you're experiencing. The burden on our shoulders is always trying to try to burden us, but ignore it and appreciate the positive aspects of your life. Your confidence and rising self-esteem lift your up. You're more competent than you thought and for that , you should be happy with yourself.

Day Twenty-Three

One thing I struggle with at times is communicating my requirements. Making the statement "I require assistance" isn't always an easy task for me. It hasn't ever been easy for me, and I don't exactly know if I'm equipped to ignore that need. I am aware that I have people who love me and want to hear my opinions However, I'm not sure what to say that I'm in need of them. This isn't something I was born with and not because I wasn't trying, but it just did not have the clarity. This could have been self-sabotage due to the fact that I didn't believe I was worthy of help, or any other kind of mental psyche that needs to be gotten out. It's likely that you are surrounded by people who would help you. You're on the road of self-development, attempting to increase your self-esteem and you've made it this far. You've made amazing progress, and you've achieved great results by yourself. Perhaps you didn't think you could do this on your own. Or perhaps you were referred to this book. Maybe you're working together with a friend or loved one. No matter what the reason for your visit, the day of day number 23 is the perfect opportunity to talk about what you're doing with someone you cherish. Contact someone, whether either a friend or family member no matter what. It's possible that it can help you more than you think. Talk about your feelings with them and let them see an aspect of you might not have previously seen. Engage and be open and they may even take the same approach and you'll realize that you share more than you imagined. In this way, you'll realize it's okay to be vulnerable and it's acceptable to have someone to chat with. Being a human, communication is an essential need, but in some way, it's become a thing that's not so much appreciated by some. It's like all of suddenly, people aren't going to discuss their feelings anymore. It could mean that you are not good enough for having feelings or being sad, however this isn't the truth. Being in a position to speak truthfully about how you feel is a virtue, do not let anyone tell you otherwise.

Day Twenty-four

As the fourth part of the course concludes, it's best to reflect on the events of the last. Together , we've covered essential and crucial notions in this section regarding mental health and the mental health. From telling yourself you're sufficient and feeling the weight and then insisting that you'll be fine. We've discussed being able to communicate when you require help , and using positive reinforcement to benefit yourself. These are all effective instruments to be on your side, however there is an additional aspect worth discussing. The most important thing is that in this section, I'll inform you that don't be listening to what voices are saying. It's not that you hear voices that advise you to do wrong things. For more precise explanation there is an internal voice telling us what we're not doing well or how much we'll fail in everything we accomplish. The voice that we hear is the worst thing to hear and it's not your friend, clearly. Everyone has it, and sometimes it wins which is almost impossible to stay clear of due to the fact that we're all humans. The feeling of unwell, it can make you feel down and you'll require assistance to move through it at times. But, remember that this isn't YOUR voice. It's not your voice and shouldn't hinder you from achieving your goals or stop you from feeling happy and improving yourself. The power is only available when you allow it to go and let it control you. It is a decision that you take each morning when you get up to make sure you don't allow it to win. Day 24 Listen to this voice and know that it isn't right. It may be there constantly, or it could be less however, know that it's not in control or constrain your potential. You're an incredible human being and you're able to achieve success in all that you accomplish. Remember that your emotional well-being is of paramount importance. It's appropriate to seek assistance. If you're feeling in need of help, ensure that you get the help you need and promptly.

Chapter 7: Yoga And Meditation

Yoga and meditation have been practiced for quite a while and are used in both secular and spiritual aspects. Yoga and meditation to build confidence in yourself.

The majority of people view yoga as the act of placing your body into a series of bent poses, and then staying still for a long period of time.

It's not true.

There are some yoga instructors who require you to keep a specific posture in order to remove the position from your mind There are many other yoga practices that require your being completely at ease. Meditation can be practiced in a variety of ways.

While some meditate where the mind has to be totally blank while others focus on an object that is a focus for meditation.

The majority of religions depend on the practice of meditation in some way. It includes praying the rosary, reading scripture passages, and reciting the chants.

Catholics, Muslims and other groups use beads from the Rosary. While meditation is seen as a as a part of Buddhism however, it is also a part of Western religious and philosophical thought. It's practiced in a different way.

For you to begin meditating the first step you need to do is commit to keep it in your practice for at minimum 30 days.

After that time and if you do not like this exercise, then put it down. However, at the very least, you should offer it an equal shot.

The first day of the week you might want to block out 10 minutes. It is possible to get in the position you prefer and allow your mind to drift into a tranquil space.

Imagine the most ideal planet, one that is packed with perfect people perfectly cooked food perfect music, perfect food, everything. It's your dream.

Make it your own. Every time you meditate and contemplate, you can talk to your inner vision during the time period you have set. time.

The key to this form of practice is it's impossible to utilize the inner utopia in by any other method. It is possible to only go to this location during meditation. This will cause you want to practice meditation every day.

What do these numbers prove? It is that, firstly you'll be able to keep the commitment. You'll need to establish an hour each day to meditate and be able follow each of them on a daily basis. If you keep practicing the art of meditation, you'll feel calm and peaceful within your body.

The majority of people who don't feel confident or have low self-esteem are not at peace with themselves. With yoga and meditation you can achieve it.

Try it. You're not risking anything and a lot to gain.

Try yoga and meditation for 10 minutes each day, and strive to achieve your personal dream of a ideal. You'll be more confident when you are able to leave your utopia knowing that your daily life will give you a sense of empowerment.

There are those who believe it's a means of "escape" the reality. It's a debate. What is more harmful retreating to a serene spot for a moment of meditation, or by escaping with several drinks? I would say the latter.

Yoga and meditation will help you relax. In the best case, they'll assist you in returning your confidence.

Chapter 8: The Benefits Of A Self-Image Positive

The advantages of having an image of self-confidence are many ... Here are a few of the main benefits.

Do More

If you've got an optimistic view it is more likely to find ways that work, as opposed to looking for reasons as to why they won't. If something isn't working in the way you expected then you've got the view to try something different without becoming frustrated. The problem won't be solved due to your optimistic outlook even if you do eventually feel somewhat down.

Get More from Others

Have you seen anyone who have a positive outlook? They are likely to have no trouble getting others to join in and are often the leader of the group. There are bound to be some negative individuals, but the majority of the group will be supportive as well as the practical.

It's better for your health

Positive thinkers are less stressed out, all else being all things being equal. If they face challenging situations, their mindset can help them overcome it faster than those who are prone to being negative. It is likely that you'll be healthier than people who have a tendency to be stressed with less stress and anxiety.

You'll Be a Much Happier Person

People tend to gravitate toward positive people even if it happens at a subconscious level. It is simply better talking with those who constantly declare. You build a network of good friends and they usually form long-lasting relationships. Some people who are not happy may continue to form friendships but they usually do never last because more people recognize that they are an annoyance to be around.

You'll be More Content

When you are able to solve more problems through positivity You are more likely to accomplish more, which will be noticed by other people. Your positive outlook will convince other people that this is not the real reason behind your actions.

With the many benefits associated with having a positive mindset The best strategy should be to put in the effort to become more positive.

It's a process that requires practice and will not occur overnight, but is worth the effort.

The benefits that come from having a good self-image is many ... Here are a few of the most significant advantages.

Do More

If you're able to have a positive view of the situation, you're more likely to identify ways to work instead of trying to figure out that they aren't. If something doesn't go in the way you expected it to, you're in the right mentality to look at other options without becoming discouraged. The problem won't be solved because of your positive outlook when you end up feeling down a bit.

Get More from Others

Have you noticed people who have a positive outlook? They probably have no problem engaging others and they are often the ones who lead of the group. There are likely to be some negative people , but the majority people in the group are supportive and supportive.

It's better for your health

Positive thinkers are less stressed with all the same points. Even when they encounter difficult situations, their outlook can help them get through it faster than those who require being negatively minded. If there's less stress within your daily life you'll likely be more healthy than people who are always exhausted.

You'll Be a Much more pleasant person

People tend to gravitate toward positive people even if it's in the subconscious. It is just easier to talk with people who always seem positive.

You'll be More Content

If you can solve more issues by being optimistic You are more likely to achieve more and be noticed by other people. Your positive outlook will convince people that this isn't your real motivation.

With all the benefits of having a positive mindset The best approach should be to always aim to become more favorable.

Self-Esteem and Psychology

Self-esteem has been a hot topic within psychology for many years and stretches the same time as psychology itself. Also, Freud which is the name that many believe was the founder of psychology (although it's not that much of a divorced father currently) has theories about self-esteem that were at the core of his work. What is self-esteem, and what it is that it creates (or isn't able to create) and what it does to it's a factor that has kept psychotherapists on the move for a lengthy time and there's no evidence that we'll be able to have everything figured out soon!

Although there's a lot that we need to find regarding self-esteem it is our belief that we at that at the very least, it had the capacity to define the definition of self-esteem and also what it differs from similar constructs. Continue reading to find out the factors that determine self-esteem in addition to other self-directed characteristics and also the definitions.

Self-Esteem vs. Self-Concept

Self-Esteem does not refer to self-concept, however, self-esteem could be part to self-concept. Self-concept refers to the view we are self-aware and our response when we have to ask the question "Who is I?" It's learning about your individual preferences, habits decisions, concepts, interests, skills and places where one is weak.

That is, the recognition of who we are is our perception of ourselves.

Purkey defines self-concept in terms of:

"the totality of a complex and well-organized and enthralling system of theories thoughts, attitudes, and points of view that everybody is able to believe in the person they are".

Based on Carl Rogers, owner of the client-centered approach, self-concept is an overall construct, and self-Esteem is one of the components of (McLeod McLeod, 2008).

Self-Esteem vs. Self-Image

Another term of similarity with different significance is self-image. Self-image is akin to self-concept in that it's everything about what you think you see yourself (McLeod in 2008). Instead of being based on reality, however it may be based on inaccurate and inaccurate ideas about the self. The image we project of ourselves could be very close to the truth, or the reverse, but it's usually not true to the facts or how we are perceived by others.

Self-esteem vs. Self-worth

Self-worth is a similar concept to self-respect , however with a small (although crucial) difference: self-esteem refers to the way we think, consider, and even believe about ourselves, while self-respect is an universal recognition that we are human beings worthy of affection.

Self-Esteem vs. Self-Efficacy

It is possible to have high self-efficacy when basketball, but you will have lower self-efficacy can be a problem when it comes to succeeding in maths courses. In contrast to self-esteem and self-efficacy, self-efficacy is more specific than global, and it is based on external accomplishment rather than internal worth.

Self- Esteem vs. Self-Compassion

Self-Esteem is not the same as self-compassion. Self-compassion may lead us to a balanced and healthy confidence in ourselves, but it's not in itself self-esteem.

Chapter 9: Great Habits To Raise Your Self-Esteem

"The most powerful connection you'll ever experience is with yourself"

- Steve Marble

What can I do to increase my self-confidence?

To boost your self-esteem it is necessary to confront and alter the negative beliefs that you hold about yourself. This might seem as if it's the most difficult task however there are plenty of possibilities to help you.

Do something you like

Engaging in activities that you love and excel at will increase your motivation and boost confidence in yourself. You can do this by offering incentives as a reward for your efforts or providing free services and care, or even an activity that you enjoy.

Work

Work can provide people a sense of identity, bonding, regular routine, and rewards. A few people thrive in an environment that is crowded and are able to appreciate the effort required to accomplish their goals. Others find work to be an unpleasant chore or work that is not paid, such as volunteering. Whatever you choose to do it is crucial that you are motivated and motivated in your work and that the harmony between your professional and family life is what you desire.

Activities for the weekend

It could be anything that involves learning another language, to singing in taking an art class. Think about where you think you possess certain natural talents or activities that you've wanted to do for many years. Find exercises that don't challenge you excessively so that you feel that you've accomplished something and have the opportunity to boost your self-esteem. The internet libraries, your local library, and the adult education schools need to provide a range of local clubs and classes you might need to go to. The thing that makes me feel more confident about myself is creating things. If I can see something I created, and am happy with it, then I feel confident about myself because I know I've discovered something that I'm good at.

Make positive connections

Find people who don't judge you and with whom you are able to talk about your feelings. If you put your energy into solid and positive people and you're sure to attain a better mental outlook and be more focused. Therefore, if you're compassionate and trustworthy to others, you're likely to receive positive reactions from them. This will make you feel confident about your own self as well as how others consider your character.

If you are self-conscious There are people around you who are a source of doubts and negative beliefs you have. It is crucial to call to these people and then take action to deter them from doing so or by gaining confidence or by limiting the length of time you communicate with them.

Find out how you can assert yourself

In assertiveness, you value yourself as much as the other people around you and communicate with respect and confidence. It helps you to set clear boundaries. The following tips will help you to take more control:

Be aware of your non-verbal communication and the words you speak Try to appear confident and confident.

* Make sure you express your emotions if you've been troubled - stay in the room until you are calm, then express your feelings clearly.

"Stop" outrageous solicitations.

• Inform people whether you require extra time or assistance with an assignment that are difficult.

Try speaking in the first person when it's applicable, such as 'When I hear you speak to me this way you am... '. This will allow you to share the things you require without appearing aggressive or terrified.

Being assertive can be a challenging skill to master it, and you might have to practice it by speaking to a mirror or someone else. A lot of adult teaching establishments such as colleges and schools, provide assertiveness training classes. There are numerous self-improvement books with exercises and suggestions that you can buy or download online.

Make sure you take care of your physical health

A healthy and balanced physical health will allow you to be more positive and useful and enhance your self-image.

Physical exercise improves sense of wellbeing and create a perception of themselves. Exercise releases endorphins which are 'feel-better hormones that enhance your mood especially when you do it outdoors.

Rest

Lack of rest could cause negative emotions to be incorrectly interpreted and make you feel less confident, therefore it is vital to ensure you are getting enough rest.

Diet

A balanced diet during your normal meal times and drinking plenty of vegetables and water will help you feel healthier and more joyful. Reducing or eliminating your alcohol consumption, and avoiding smoking and recreational drugs will also help increase the general health of your.

Challenge yourself

If you set your own goals and strive to achieve them, you'll be happy and content for yourself when you hit your goal. You will feel more confident about your self.

Be sure the test you have set for yourself is attainable and easily achievable. It's not required that it be a major issue, but it should be important to you. For instance, you could decide to compose an email to the local newspaper or start taking a daily fitness class.

Find out how you can be aware of and contest negative convictions

If you boost confidence in yourself, it could be a good opportunity to reveal your negative perceptions about yourself and the places they originate. It can be a difficult process, therefore it's important to take your time and possibly seek out a friend or partner to assist you. If you're struggling and need help, it might be beneficial to seek out expert advice from a professional advisor who can help you to accomplish this. It can be beneficial to keep a record of notes and ask questions for instance they can help you keep your thoughts in order:

What do you believe are your flaws or shortcomings?

What negative things do you think others consider about you?

* If you had to summarize the meaning of the word, what would you use to describe "I have... "?

* When did it start experiencing this sensation?

* Can you describe an incident or event that could have triggered this condition?

* Do you notice that your thoughts are negative every day?

It can also be helpful to keep a journal of ideas or write down your thoughts over a period of time. Note down the specifics of what happened and how you felt and what you believe the root of your conviction was.

Focus on positive things. If you're struggling with low self-esteem, it may be difficult to get used to thinking positively about yourself. One way to achieve this is creating a list of a handful of things you appreciate about yourself. You can include:

• Things that describe your character

• Things to consider about how you appear

* Things you can do

* Skills that you have developed.

Make sure to take your time and look for 50 different items, regardless of whether it's a long process. Keep the list in mind and look at each day. Take a look at a different item each day. If you're feeling low or overwhelmed by an event coming up such as an upcoming employee meeting or a potential employee meet-up, this list can be used to remind you of the positive aspects of yourself. If you are struggling to come up with the most valuable things you can request your partner or friend to help you begin.

It can also aid you to see how other people might have a better opinion of yourself than yourself. Another option is to write down at least three positive things you did or things you done that day prior to taking a get to bed. Many people also believe that it's a good idea to keep items such as photos or even letters, that look look like the objects.

Try mindfulness techniques

Mindfulness is a way of staying focused on the present moment by using methods such as meditation breath, yoga, and meditation. It has been proven to assist people in becoming more aware of their thoughts and feelings so that rather than being overwhelmed by them, it's easier to manage their behavior.

What can your loved ones do to assist?

If you know someone who lack self-esteem There are a variety of alternatives you can take.

Let them know that you value them - tell to them that you'll respect and cherish them. It is possible to show them what you are feeling by being kind and attentive or spending time with them.

Help them remember positive things. While you are unable to change someone's negative image of them, you can to change this perception by helping them be aware of the great things they have done such as amazing things or positive things they've done.

Refrain from blaming other people Self-esteem sufferers frequently accuse themselves of having bad experiences, and this includes problems with their mental well-being. Remind them that this isn't their fault and refrain from encouraging them to pull themselves together.'

Try to remain persistent. self-esteem issues typically develop over a period of time. Redefining someone's view of himself or herself may take a long time and may require frequent consolation.

Inform them that it's acceptable to be miserable occasion, everyone is not satisfied and motivated all the time and it is vital that to not feel pressured to satisfy their naive desires.

If your friend or relative is taking part in a self-improvement plan or is working with an advisor, you should be encouraging and encouraging. It is also possible to offer help, for instance, giving them childcare so that they can attend meetings.

Encourage them to seek the right treatment. If you're worried that your low self-esteem could be creating a psychological health problem or a family member, encourage your friend or a friend to seek the right treatment.

Self-improvement and self-improvement materials

Be aware of these tips that will help you to boost your self-esteem.

Do exercises you enjoy.

* Enjoy time with positive and steady people.

Be kind and considerate to people around you.

Try not to be a comparison to other people.

* Make sure you do regular exercise, eat well and rest enough.

* Be clear - don't give people an opportunity to treat you disrespectfully.

Utilize self-improvement guidebooks and websites to develop an understanding of support like assertiveness or mindfulness.

• Learn to challenge your convictions.

• Recognize your positive qualities and the things you excel at.

* Develop the habit of remembering and exclaiming positive things about yourself.

Why is Self-Esteem crucial?

Self-esteem refers to people's beliefs about their self-worth and value. It also deals with the feelings people feel that differ in their perception of their worthiness or disdain. Self-esteem is important as it influences people their choices and decisions. Self-esteem can be a source of inspiration because it makes it more likely for individuals to take care of themselves and explore their potential. People who have high self-esteem are more inclined in taking care of themselves and work toward achieving their own goals and aspirations. Self-esteem sufferers generally do not believe that they are worthy of great results or as suited to achieve them, and thus tend to allow things to slide and are less determined and adaptable in beating obstacles. They might have their own particular goals, similar to those with more self-esteem, but they're generally less motivated to follow them to their final destination.

Chapter 10: Self-Respect

Self-respect is an entirely distinct thing from respect. Simply put self-respect is more of an internal issue. It's not visible on the surface, however the results are noticeable. It is something you do for yourselfand the result is that it radiates out to other people. Self-respect is a derived term that comes from respect from the English dictionary however it's actually reversed. Understanding the basic aspects of respect is helpful in the practice of self-respect, which includes what respect means.

Respect

The first definition of respect was consider or to'regard.' The word has since been broadened its meaning to encompass definitions like 'to be treated with deference,' respect with dignity and respect or 'to be fearful of.' The former is utilized within a different setting, such as the realm of religion or when it comes to authority. Respect typically has two components which are both a subject and an object. They can be interchangeable dependent on the side we are looking from. The subject reacts to the object in a manner that is either without or with regard, while the object displays the same reaction. The response of the subject is how they feel or react to an object's presence, and toward the actions objects do. Respect can be expressed in many ways that include beliefs, judgements and acknowledgments emotions, moods, motives, and attitudes.

There are a variety of ways to can be used to determine the amount of respect which is shown to the object. This is a good basis for you in your efforts to develop self-esteem. You are both the subject and object of your self.

Appearance- this is a type of cognition in which the subject considers the surrounding and the physical characteristics and features of an object. The subject determines how they will act and react to these attributes and in general towards the object.

* Appraisal - the subject evaluates the object's merit. This is influenced by factors such as the

title and the age of the object. In normal circumstances the subject wouldn't show the object this level of respect if not because of their position. This makes this type of respect superficial. It is not real, but the object may not even notice the difference for while the status quo is maintained.

* Position- This kind of respect differs from appraisal in the sense how the subject is treated in indirect manner. In the context of institutions, for instance the people who hold higher positions are respected because they adhere to the rules and regulations of the institution. This type of respect will usually extend beyond the boundaries of the institution. Consider a situation where spouse and husband work in the same business. The spouse is the manager, and the husband is an entry-level employee. The wife will receive special respect in the workplace however, this may not be evident when they leave for home in the evening. Respect doesn't stop there however, it does take another level.

* Required respect- the person must pay the subject respect regardless of. This is usually seen

in military settings where junior officers have to demonstrate respect for their senior officers by obeying direct and indirect commands. This could also be thought of as indirect respect as the goal is to follow guidelines set by the organization; it's more about respecting the rules or instructions rather than the one that came up in conjunction with them.

Respect for barriers- this is the respect shown to objects that are considered to be obstacles by the subject. The subject simply shows respect when they attempt to get over these barriers because they could be hurt in the event that they fail to do so. An excellent example of this is driving a jeep in an area of park and meet a group of lions at the side of the highway. You must drive carefully to avoid the ferocious animals or risk getting ripped into pieces.

Respect for the character - it is the most genuine and appropriate form of respect. It's all about the way that the subject conducts their behavior in the presence of the other. The subject is able to examine the character of the object before deciding the amount of respect they will show.

But, even if this kind of respect appears genuine, it is also disproved by the object in particular in the case of achieving specific goals.

* Core Respect

* This is a respect for the inherent and natural traits of you. It is more than just doing what is right. It's a determination to establish an ethical way of life every single day. It also means remaining in a position of absolute conviction and adhering to your core values in all circumstances. Certain of these rules are universally applicable to people with character. The core value of respect is embedded within these people. These include:

Integrity is the ability to stand by your personal convictions and beliefs, by adhering to your heart and refusing to be subdued. It is also about being upright and strong. Someone who is honest adheres to their principles regardless of what others say about them. They are vigilant about their reputation regardless of how costly it appear. They aren't doing anything wrong to please others nor attempt to obtain what they need at the expense other people. It's the most effective way of building self-esteem.

* Courtesy- People will always be able to do to you what they do to you. Being courteous is being respectful and polite with people. There is no respect for a person who treats people in a way that is discriminatory, such as making fun of, ridiculing or humiliating them. A person who is courteous is one who is respectful of themselves.

* Tolerance, which means accepting people for what they are, without judging them according to gender, ability or beliefs. It is also about being able to consider the opinions of others just as you'd like you to hear theirs. Someone who lacks respect will make use of every chance they have to judge and discriminate against people.

* Loyalty- This refers to the capacity and the willingness to stand up for the people you value or are friends with, including colleagues, friends, and family members. Being there to protect them and protect their interests when they're threatened. A trustworthy person will guard the secrets of those closest to them. They will never

lie to people who are who are close to them, nor do they let them commit wrong actions that could harm their reputation. They do not backbite or behave self-centered in front of their loved ones.

Honesty- the core value requires being able to tell the truth, even if it turns against you. Believing, deceiving or stealing will cause more harm than the negative consequences of being honest. People will be impressed when you're honest and honest at all times. This shows them that you are more concerned about your dignity than anything else.

Diplomacy- being diplomatic means that you are able to solve disputes peacefully and with fairness. Diplomacy means that you are able to resolve issues without resorting to violence and without being predisposed. This is a quality only the best of characters possess. People who are not respected can let their anger take over when they face disputes. They'll use violence and threats to get their way. This only creates negative images of their fundamental respect and they won't get respect as well.

* Reliability: The ability to stick to your word is an important boost to respect. This means that you are reliable and reliable. It is the opposite of someone who always strays from their word, or is not faithful to their promises and promises. A person like this is unattractive and indicates an absence of respect for the core.

Personal Rules

Here are some Dos and Don'ts that will help you live your daily life. You take them with you wherever you travel. Making personal rules as well as observing them are two distinct things. It's more difficult to follow the rules that you've created in comparison to those created by somebody else. It requires dedication and perseverance to stick to the rules you have set for yourself. However, you will not be able to lead an extraordinary life without these guidelines. Following the rules you've made implies that your self-esteem is greater than. A few of these rules are listed below.

Make a plan for your day prior to when you get started with anything. This allows you to keep things in order and complete everything you need to do during the day. It also ensures that you don't spend your time doing nothing and get caught up in negative thoughts instead of engaging in worthwhile things. The best method to organize your schedule is to create a an agenda which covers all 24 hours. It is important to ensure that everything is scheduled sufficient time.

Create a steady sleeping routine. Do not be the type of person who can get into to and out at any time you'd like. Make sure you go to bed and get up the same time each day. This will not only help you establish a regular sleep routine, but helps you stick to your schedule that you've created when making your plans for the day. If you adhere to this rule it implies that you will not be rushing or rushing through tasks. When you create your sleeping schedule, make sure that you allow enough time for rest that is around eight hours per day.

Take time for yourself throughout the day. Be aware it is you who are the main element of these guidelines; it's all about you. Your physical self must be cared for by doing exercising and surveillance. Your mental health requires attention through meditation to relieve anxiety and stress. Your emotional self needs to be examined by the process of soul-searching and tracking your feelings. Make time for these tiny daily routines every day, and these tasks are only an hour in your day. In this time, block off all distractions, including social media until you're finished.

* Make an effort to appreciate every person you meet before your day is over. Be grateful to those who have done the smallest of things for you during the day. An easy smile or "thank you" is sufficient when someone does kindness. If you're religious, then show gratitude to God for the blessings of life each morning when you leave bed , and then immediately before going to sleep. Create this a daily habit and you will see the way you live life you'll live.

You should make your bed every day when you awake. Get started on your charity right in your bedroom. It's a simple task that holds a significant importance for your plans for the day. Making your bed in a neat and tidy manner is the first sign that you're ready to start your day with a well-organized way.

Concordance

This is the need to achieve your goals and goals not because someone wants you to, but because you think they are in line with your core desires. This is a kind of self-motivation, which is crucial in fostering self-respect. Self-concordant people have more subjective wellbeing. However those who lack self-concordance are not as effective in performing tasks, whether for themselves or in their places of work. Concordance can lead to happiness since the self-concordant will always employ their own methods and strategies for achieving their goals. This approach is efficient because it is accepted by the individual in contrast to established practices which tend to be rigid. This type of satisfaction comes from respect for your goals and interests. Self-respecting people feel obligated to follow those goals until the finish without pressure. This produces astonishing outcomes for the individual.

Boundaries

These are the rules and limits which must be observed to ensure your relationship with others and yourself. There are boundaries that you establish that cannot be crossed by other people There are boundaries which others have drawn and you are not allowed to violate them. Boundaries are more of a warning and can be a source of punishment should they be crossed. These boundaries protect interest of two sides who draw them as well as the one that is not supposed to cross. Boundaries are essential as they protect our self-respect and ensure that we're protected from harm, and allows us to express our desires to others, establish boundaries in our relationships and also ensure that we have enough spaces and our time.

Boundary Boxes

Like the Plassom Meter Boundary Box, self-respect boundary boxes are designed to shield you from external threats. This box will ensure that you are in a safe and a healthy environment to grow and nourish yourself. The boundary is not visible physically, however it is visible because you've communicated it to those who are around you. They are more of a mental boundaries. They include the following:

Convictions, beliefs or personal opinions define the boundaries of thoughts you're required to think about. It's hard to know if the boundaries exist until you cross it. If you find that your thoughts are going beyond your identity and more specifically towards negative thoughts, put an end to them right away. Put the thing that is negative on hold and switch your attention to something more positive.

* Values- Your fundamental values define the person you develop into. Be sure to guard them with aplomb and do not compromise them in any way. Any value you consider positive should be embraced However, put a stop to anything that is contrary to what you believe in.

* Opinions - not every opinion is worth a listen. If an idea threatens your self-esteem, however appealing it may sound, stay clear of it

completely. You should only allow ideas that can build your mind.

Boundary ranges

This is the length of your boundaries. This is the process of setting an elastic limit on each border. If the limit is exceeded and you are unable to meet it, then your self-esteem is at risk. It's fine to allow individuals, thoughts as well as other items, however, only to a specific limit. It is possible to, for instance permit someone to contribute their opinions on a topic that you both are interested in, but should you find that their opinions are in conflict with your own, then put an end to it. The boundary is violated. Now it's about them and not you.

Boundary levels

This is the degree of your relationship with yourself or other people. It's about the capacity to accept only what you can accept. Learn to differentiate your emotions from the feelings of others to be protected from being manipulated and losing your self-esteem while doing it. Allowing your emotions to be influenced by the opinions and thoughts will make you feel pressured to satisfy them. Recognize when the boundary is crossed and respond in a timely manner.

Boundary circles

These physical boundaries are put in place to safeguard your body and space from being violated. When these boundaries are crossed, one is vulnerable to discrimination. In a sense, this is your fault since those boundaries were never intended to be violated. To ensure your self-esteem be aware of who's supposed to touch you, when they're supposed to touch you, and the location where they're supposed to be touching you. Anyone who does not respect your privacy is crossing a line. Anyone who does not touch you in the right area has crossed a border. Someone who is touching you in a manner that causes you to feel uncomfortable also has crossed a line.

The Remote Control on your remote

To be self-confident, you must learn to manage various aspects of your life with the click of the button. Find out when you should switch things off or on in accordance with the impact they're having on your inner being.

* Negative thoughts shouldn't be allowed to remain in your head for long. Make sure to hit that power-off button as soon as you will be able to identify them. After that, you can switch on beautiful and positive thoughts that can strengthen you. It is possible to switch between different thoughts by changing channels. If an idea is old and uninteresting, switch to a fresh idea which is pertinent to the current circumstance.

* The remote control you have allows you to regulate your emotions. If your relationship is headed to the south, say it is best to reduce the emotional ties to the relationship by pressing the button to turn down the volume. This will spare you from suffering and will ensure that you are respected when the relationship ends. Also, increase your feelings when you are in an opportunity to be in a relationship.

Control the volume in the event that you are listening to other people's opinions. It should be turned off when you feel negative and then turn it back on when you see positive.

Assertiveness

This means that you can remain firm while accepting the views of others. Being able to maintain that balance doesn't just increase the amount of respect you are given however, it also demonstrates that you've earned a high self-esteem. Being assertive is a win-win for everyone in which both parties walk out with their confidence intact. It is a great method of protecting one's self-esteem. It is possible to practice assertiveness by adhering to these rules;

Know what you are looking for before negotiations begin. This means being aware of your rights and interests. Inform the other party of your needs and be aware of the reaction. Be sure to clearly communicate this to drive your idea into the forefront.

* Make sure you can say it NOW it is required and then justify why you're making that decision, and ensure that your explanation is positive.

Open to critique in the same way that you are open to praises.

Try to determine what the interests of the other side are. It may not be easy to discern however you can get them to clarify and allow them to present their position without judgement or interruption.

Be sure to weigh each side and be careful not to be swayed by bias. Being biased on one side can make you less self-confident. Even if you won as because of your bias and losing the respect of your opponent side and your own respect.

Testing Boundaries

The quality of the boundaries you establish can only be assessed by conducting tests on the boundaries. This must be carried out in a controlled way to prevent things from spiralling out of reach of. The testing of boundaries helps you find and close gaps. It can also help you come up with suitable measures to take action when boundaries are breached.

Skills to Create better Boundaries

To establish boundaries, you need to have the right skills to ensure that they are not easily broken. These skills include:

Be aware of where you start and where you'll end. This will allow you to keep track of your boundaries without difficulty.

It is important to separate your identity from others. This gives you the chance to determine what is right for you and what's not. Also, it protects your from competition that is harmful.

You are completely responsible for yourself. The quality of your boundaries determines how much security you receive.

• Overcome guilt, shame and self-centeredness prior to making a decision about boundaries. This will clear your thoughts and helps you to be more assertive when protecting your boundaries.

Be supportive and reward individuals who adhere to your boundaries. Rebuke people who don't respect them. This lets you only connect with those who value and respect you.

Healthy Relationship

This is a partnership where your rights and interests are considered. It's a relationship in which the right to define limits is not considered to be selfish. A healthy relationship allows you to build self-esteem because the other person respects your character and is willing to give you credit for it. They will later reciprocate in the same way. A lack of self-esteem however it will expose you to unhealthy relationships in which nobody respects you. These are some tips to ensure you creating an enduring relationship.

Learn to listen another person in the similar way you want them to listen to you.

* Don't be quick to make a judgement. Consider you in their shoes before making a decision.

Accept your mistakes and be open to criticism.

* Don't prioritize your needs over the interests of your partner. Make sure you have a sense of

balance so that you don't end up being seen as greedy and selfish.

Respect the boundaries of others If you want yours to be respect.

Chapter 11: What You Can Do To Enhance Self-Esteem

You're what you think of yourself. If you do not feel that you are worthy of the attributes you possess then you won't feel confident about yourself. You're not confident in yourself.

What is the difference between self-esteem and self-acceptance? Aren't they the same? Do they not have the identical significance? Do they not have to refer to the way you perceive yourself?

Self-Acceptance vs. Self-Esteem

Both terms are similar, but they are not identical. Self-esteem refers to the value you think you are, whereas self-acceptance refers to your acceptance of your strengths as a person. What's more important is self-esteem or self-acceptance?

Self-acceptance is more crucial to grow than self-esteem. You build self-esteem through the actions you take and the possessions you own. In today's world of celebrity-driven culture many people associate self-esteem with youth, fame, and riches; this is a superficial form of self-esteem. What happens when you're no longer famous? What happens when you're older than you are or if you don't have enough money? You lose your self-esteem? Many people fall victim to this.

Self-acceptance is, however is accepting who you are, both the good things as well as the negative while being content about it. When you have complete self-acceptance that you are content with where you are, regardless of whether you're rich or are living in the midst of poverty.

If you are able to accept yourself as well, your self-esteem is likely to increase. When you stop thinking about yourself as not attractive enough, not being sexy enough or because you aren't wealthy enough, then you'll be able to feel more confident in your self-image.

What determines self-acceptance?

When you are a child as a child, you're only in a position to accept yourself in the same way that your parents have accepted you. There is evidence to suggest that prior to the age of eight, children they are unable to discern clearly and create the identity of a person from other from what their parents and caregivers transmit to them. That is If your parents have fed them with ideas that you're good, and, even though you're flawed, you're an amazing creation that is a gift from God and you'll not be able to accept your own shortcomings as you get older.

In the media-driven world we reside in, you will find many beauty-enhancing cosmetics and surgical procedures that are marketed to look beautiful. Beauty is now synonymous with skinny and sexy, so for instance, if are an extra-large person one, you must cut the fat that is accumulating around you. If your teen was raised in a family environment which valued them regardless of imperfections, he/she will not be able to overcome the challenges of gaining confidence in themselves.

But, if you were told that you were not good enough in your teen years You will end into a person who believes that you're not worthy of anything and your self-esteem as well as self-acceptance will be affected.

What you experienced as a teenager won't be forgotten; therefore when you're a parent it's the way you've been taught and the cycle continues to grow.

How to Be More Self-Asserting

Accepting yourself and loving unconditionally is not difficult if your parents taught you this way. But, if they communicated another message, that's where the problem lies.

But, it's never enough to make a change in how you view yourself. If you've never felt satisfaction in your life, be able to meet your challenge to become completely to fully accept yourself.

If you've had a bad experience day, this is your opportunity to alter the way you be. There's a level of happiness that is related to the level of self-acceptance. You'll be happier in the event that you believe that you have the right to be content. Many people don't feel peaceful and happiness in their lives due to the fact that they believe they aren't worthy to be.

Self-Compassion and Self-Acceptance

To gain self-acceptance, it may require you to work on self-compassion. When you're able to acknowledge your flaws and weaknesses or forgive any mistakes made, you is more comfortable for you to be accepting of yourself. When you practice compassion, you come to realize that you're not that terrible after all, even though you may have making a number of wrongs in your past.

To become more self-accepting, you need to avoid negative thoughts. Re-examine the feelings of guilt, inadequacy and self-criticisms. Find out what you do not like about yourself. Then, begin to heal yourself by accepting your imperfections and flaws. Begin to appreciate your strengths as well as the positive things about yourself.

The Fundamentals of Self-Acceptance

To be able to accept yourself to be accepted by others, there are a few fundamentals to be aware of.

Overcome Fear

In order to achieve confidence in yourself, you must to be able to change the way you perceive yourself. This is accomplished by changing your beliefs regarding your self-image.

The majority of people who were raised being a victim have this fundamental conviction about themselves: that they're not good enough. They believe they're not attractive enough and worthy of being loved. The notion of not being beautiful enough is based on their appearance and how smart they have, or the amount of money they make.

Another major belief is that people have to attain a certain amount of success to build a positive self-image. Many people are influenced by an untrue sense of happiness and success: fame and money.

The process of changing these beliefs can be difficult, particularly when you've been taught this sort of belief.

These two fundamental beliefs are the primary cause of your fear. You must alter the way in which you perceive your self based on these beliefs to overcome that feeling of fear.

Do not be a perfectionist!

What is the best thing to do? Are you a perfectionist? Being a perfectionist can be beneficial in certain ways. If you're a perfectionist, then you are serious about your work; you make sure that you do you can when working on any project for your business.

Are you an obsessive perfectionist in all areas in your daily life? In particular, you seek a perfect marriage, which is why, even if you have a person you like and who you love back. But, due to reasons only you can determine you decide to not seek out. You wish the perfect relationship and so you look for someone who is perfect, because you think you are perfect.

If your self-conception of perfection makes you struggle to accept your own self-worth, then you've got the lowest self-esteem. You strive to be a good person every single thing you do to ensure that when things don't occur as you'd like it to you don't get too hard on yourself. You believe that if you do your best to achieve perfection, you will get there.

You are prone to "reject" yourself because you aren't "perfect" This means that your self-esteem suffers. You believe it is the only method to achieve self-acceptance is to strive to be perfect. It is easy to "reject" yourself because you aren't adequate because you can't attain perfection in all that you accomplish.

The idea of perfection needs to be put down. It is important to recognize that no one can be flawless. You can put in the effort to achieve anything, but only to a certain degree however it won't be 100% perfect. Every single thing has weaknesses and drawbacks; this is things work. To have an enlightened view of self-acceptance that you must admit that you're not perfect and that in spite of your imperfections, you're adequate.

There is No Self-Rejection When You Feel Confident in Yourself

Many people are conditioned by the belief that happiness can only be achieved through absolute excellence. It is believed that success is synonymous with confidence. This is the reason some people are unable to be convinced that they must let go of their ideal image in order to gain confidence and self-acceptance.

Many associate the feeling of happiness with the feeling of security that comes from having achieved success. But having success doesn't mean your mental state will change. Attaining a certain amount of success doesn't mean that the way you think about your self will alter. There are those that have reached the peak of their accomplishment, but acknowledge that they are not fulfilled and unsatisfied.

An euphoric moment can cause you to feel happy for a moment, but the feeling will not last forever. After the emotion has subsided and you return to the fundamental conviction that you're not enough. Then you return to that feeling of being judged of the actions you take. It is returning to setting a new goals and the current level of success isn't quite enough.

Change Your Mind About What You Believe

If you're looking to increase your self-confidence, you must get rid of the notion that you're not enough or don't deserve the great things that happen to you. These beliefs and thoughts trigger feelings of anxiety. Although the emotions aren't an issue however, the effects and consequences of holding onto negative beliefs are.

If you've been told that you're not good enough, this is the image that is left in your mind. This image will also take form in you.

It is important to realize that the self-image you create of yourself isn't what you are in reality "real self". Change your perspective by moving away from the flawed enough self-image you've constructed for yourself.

You're not your image. Image You Created

Your mind may mislead you about how to perceive your self-image. Sometimes , the mind creates an image of yourself that is intended to boost your self-esteem and ultimately gain self-acceptance. but, it is possible to make a false self-image since it reinforces an imagined image of perfect.

All it boils down to is changing your beliefs in the first place as that will alter the image you created over the years. The image your mind has fed you must be altered now since this doesn't represent your "real person you are".

If you create a ideal self-image, you'll not be able to accept your real self with all of your imperfections.

Self-Acceptance Guide

Self-acceptance isn't a requirement that requires the use of step-by-step methods. Your self-image came from your mind. It originated within your own self, so the process of gaining self-acceptance should be rooted in the deepest parts of your own being.

People always strive for something

Human nature makes us desire items that bring you happiness. Do you have a black dress that you've always desired? Do you regularly go to the store where your dream automobile is on display? Have you ever thought of having your own house? Perhaps you're hoping to meet your ideal person? Think about this: if you could have all these, would end up happy and content?

People believe that if they get famous, powerful and rich, they'll be content and content. However, if you attain this status, would you truly be content? Are you able to love yourself completely?

Consider the wealthy and famous who find themselves being lonely or living in a solitary home. They have everything they've ever imagined but aren't content.

If you've been living in a state of depreciation and insecurity, nothing or fame will alter how you view yourself. There is always some gap and you'll always be striving to do better than you due to the fact that despite the money you've earned but you're not enough and you want to earn more in order to attain the level of perfection. It is actually an illusion of self-esteem.

Change must come from within.

If you are looking to alter your fundamental beliefs and eventually achieve self-acceptance, you need begin changing your mindset. There is no one who can do it for you, and you should not let anyone decide what kind of person you'll become.

Here's a brief guide on how to build self-acceptance

* You have to determine the points of contention that you are unable to take into consideration.

If you're unable to identify the root of the negative image you have of yourself It will be difficult to achieve complete self-acceptance. Do you have a part of your life you are not happy with? Are you content with your work? Are you in a steady relationship with your spouse? Are you in top health?

In what aspects of your existence are you the most content? Which are you unhappy with?

Self-acceptance is about yourself, being happy and accepting what you have. It should not be concerned with what others consider your self-esteem. It should be about how you perceive yourself.

Self-acceptance is about your self-esteem! Do not try to please everyone until you are damaging your self-image. Remember that no matter how well you behave, will always have a way to criticize your character.

* Be aware of the positive aspects of your character.

Once you have a clear picture of the things you don't like about yourself, it's time to find the things that make you feel happy in your life. Find your strengths. Find your strengths and strong areas. Consider what people think of you , and what you appreciate about you.

Negative thoughts shouldn't remain in your thoughts or in your life. They're silent killers and can consume you from the inside. If you're determined to improve your life and feel more comfortable with yourself start by looking for the positives in your life beginning by focusing on your thinking.

Focus your attention focus on the positive aspects. Are you unhappy with how you appear? If you have something you aren't happy about on your appearance, acknowledge that you are imperfect and that's a part of you. there's no way to change it other than to accept it as it is. Instead of dwelling on the things that don't look good you, think about what looks attractive within your own. Are you blessed with a stunning pair of eyes? Or do you have stunning hair?

Your appearance is only the surface of the iceberg. When you're able to be aware of the good you have in yourself regardless of how people perceive you. It must come from the inside. Feel beautiful inside, and you'll radiate that beauty to the world outside. And you're only beginning.

Make a list of the minimum of ten qualities you are proud of about yourself, physical or emotional, however. You could love something that you have or how you lookor your talents. Write them down and you will feel happy to know that you've got these great things about yourself. When you feel that you're not doing well and you're feeling low check your list and remind yourself that there are plenty of positive aspects of your life.

• Create an action plan to remove all negatives from your life.

It is crucial to develop an a plan of action that can be executed. It is going to be a battle with emotions as well as readjusting behavior patterns , which can be a very difficult task. But, with determination and perseverance you'll be able to turn things back around and be successful.

It could be a matter of the process of trial and error until you have found the perfect method. Be prepared for difficulties as there won't be absolute perfection immediately, so it's crucial to begin with baby steps. Start with action plans can be completed in the span of a week, and you will be able to improve the plans you have in place as you go along.

It may be a better option to seek help by a professional counselor to help you get back on track. Self-acceptance is an important aspect in making changes in your life.

It's a process, that is not a quick fix. As you progress through the process, you'll observe several changes in your behaviour when you build confidence in yourself. Your self-image will gradually change, and in time, you'll begin to be able to see yourself as the "real self". As time passes you'll recognize the positive things you possess and be wondering why you didn't view yourself in that way prior to now.

The process of gaining self-acceptance doesn't end there but it's an ongoing process. As you develop as an individual, you'll learn new things about yourself. If you remain on the right track you shouldn't have an issue.

Chapter 12: The Role Of Forgiving

Imagine for the moment that you're on a staircase. The staircase is the way to reach a goal. As you walk along the staircase, in the middle you've made an error. What do you do? Do you rise and continue to move ahead? Or do you decide to take a tumble down the stairs and ruin the progress you've achieved in achieving your target?

If you are not able to accept the mistakes you made by self-sabotaging, you're self-sabotaging. The consequences of mistakes can be frustration, sadness anger, guilt, and sadness. All of these feelings are negative and uncomfortable. Although experiencing them after making a mistake is normal and normal, lingering over these feelings only makes you more miserable. If you commit a misstep and are unable to let it go you're causing yourself suffering and negative feelings in order to undermine yourself.

Be aware that you are human. Expect not to avoid mistakes. There isn't one living individual who has never made a mistake during their life. There are mistakes made by people as early as they are young and all they can do is learn from their mistakes. Consider the number of cups toddlers have to spill before they are able to drink from the cup. The cups are all messes, but without those mistakes the toddler would not have had the chance to drink from a cup.

Strategies to Forgive Yourself

It is much easier to say than it is to do. While it is more comfortable to accept forgiveness for yourself (and others) as you get more comfortable but it can be difficult initially. These methods can help you let forget your mistakes much simpler:

You must separate yourself from past experiences. Everyone's story is an individual story and some are more difficult than others. If you're struggling with a mistake within your own past, the most effective method to let yourself forgive yourself is to concentrate on making changes. If you're so angry by your behavior that it's making you feel ill right now, you can try to separate yourself from the previous mistakes. Keep in mind that at any point you are able to alter how you behave and become more of a person. This is not possible when you're constantly thinking about your past self. Instead, strive to become the best version of you.

You should be able to recognize your strengths. A boost in confidence when you make an error helps you appreciate your strengths and counterbalance your weak points. This is especially helpful where you've excelled in something, but failed in a similar field. For example, whereas one may fail in cooking bacon in the first attempt but they could have a very good taste and are adept at mixing spices. They're not bad in the kitchen, but they require a bit more training in specific areas.

• Make mistakes in the process of learning. Forgiveness is essential since it is detrimental to trust your judgement too excessively. Studies show that those who have a high degree of expertise in their area (like medical professionals) have a lower chance to recognize and rectify errors because they think their judgement is sound. If you're open to errors, it provides you with an increased chance of recognizing and resolving the issue before it becomes serious issues. Furthermore by being willing to making mistakes, you're giving yourself the chance to test your self-confidence, without worrying about the consequences.

Try to approach the situation with an open-minded approach. If you're exploring something new, it could be stressful or be enjoyable. Instead of worrying about if you'll do it right try it out as an experiment. Make yourself promise yourself that you're planning to attend the class in yoga or work with a renowned client, to test the waters. While failure could be an option, it's much more likely to be the opportunity to learn.

* Block away the complainers. Sometimes the mistakes we make can result in us being held responsible by others. If you can't convince someone else to forgive your mistakes, it's essential to accept forgiveness for yourself. The act of holding grudges back does nothing to encourage positivity in your life. Instead of being concerned about how the world is reacting,

realize that you're still a work in progress. It is normal to make mistakes and those who expect that you are flawless are the kind of people who create stress in your life.

* Pay attention to patterns. It is common for mistakes to are a part of every other aspect of life. It is beneficial to keep a record of your successes and failures. In keeping track of those mistakes made, you have an opportunity to discover which areas you're successful in and what areas you'll should improve. When you track your achievements you can determine what strategies have proven successful. Your accomplishments also give you the opportunity to take a break from making mistakes, and help you keep a clear view of what you're capable of accomplishing.

* Learn more. If you're unable to actively let yourself be sorry for mistakes, then take the initiative to forgive yourself by learning and practicing. Find out more about a technique by conducting research or asking a friend to help. Learning the skills that led you to make mistakes will assist you in forgiveness. If you notice how

you're becoming proficient at something, the mistakes will appear less significant.

Find out the root cause for the error. Sometimes, discovering the cause to the mistake could assist you in avoiding having the same issue next time. Imagine, for example, you've made acquaintances with some one. After a few weeks your friend informs you that the person is not trustworthy. You believe in your judgement and they take your money. The blame lies with the behavior of their accomplices, not on yours. While you may want to be less at risk in the future it's important to keep in mind that, at the time you were acting with a limited awareness. You were acting in a responsible manner based on the information you were given at the time.

• Talk about yourself in a way as were your best friend. Although we frequently make ourselves feel guilty for our own shortcomings it's much harder to critique the actions of those whom you cherish. If someone is too critical of themselves it's helpful to imagine that you are someone you cherish. Take a look at how you would help them through their mistakes and what advice you'd give them. You can then give yourself that identical guidance.

Accept the responsibility. Making amends for mistakes is much easier when you're held responsible for the actions you took. Before you can forgive yourself and accept the responsibility of what you did. Remind people that you apology and develop an action plan to change. It is impossible to correct mistakes already committed. However, you can make changes to your behavior to the next time around. Forgiveness from the other people affected can be beneficial particularly if you've offended or hurt anyone in some way.

Re-evaluate your morals and values. If you are unable to let yourself go, think about the values that are the most crucial to you. How do you plan to portray yourself ? How do you intend to behave? If your actions don't align with your ideals Perhaps it is an opportunity to reconsider the choices you're making in your life. If you do this, you could eventually be in a position to accept the forgiveness you deserve.

Do yourself a favor and give yourself a "do-over'. Doing it again gives you an chance to get it correctly. Of of course, there are circumstances where it is impossible to recreate the exact scenario. Imagine what transpired and note down what you could have different. When you do this, you're proving that you've learned the lessons learned from the error. Also, you're learning a better way to handle similar situations in the future.

Forgiveness is an essential part of building self-confidence and self-esteem. If you're incapable of accepting yourself as you are and your mistakes, you're also incapable of learning from your mistakes. Doing nothing to alleviate negative emotions will not alter the past. Moving forward and letting go of your past with the right strategies allows you to improve.

Chapter 13: Empathy

We refer to empathy as the ability to place oneself in the shoes of someone else, and to comprehend the thoughts and feelings other people are experiencing and how the circumstances or our actions impact them. It's about seeing things without judging them objectively or coldly however, seeing them in the way the person who experiences them is what implications do they have for the person as well as their personality, surroundings, and context and their individuality and quirks.

Empathy is an essential component of deep interpersonal relationships along with emotional and interpersonal intelligence, allowing us to have an adequate and flexible interaction with others , as well as the control of our own emotions as well as the awareness of the emotions of others in our world. The absence of empathy can cause problems on the daily life of the person lacking it as well as in its surrounding environment, creating anxiety, loneliness and problems with adapting to society or surveillance of social standards.

There are many reasons that lead to a lack of empathy, ranging from lack of affection in childhood, to experiencing physical, psychological, and sexual abuse. It can also be passed through various images and neurodevelopmental, neurological, or psychological issues. It is crucial to remember that everyone is unique and their abilities are different. empathy is slightly or significantly developed every one of us. However, the complete lack of empathy is a challenge and typically occurs in various disorders.

The signs that indicate the absence of empathy

1. Introspection within oneself

One characteristic that people who suffer from an absence of empathy typically share, particularly those with autism The feeling is that they are focusing only on themselves and are not completely aware of those surrounding them.

2. Understanding problems

Being unable to place oneself in the shoes of other people makes it hard for those with difficulties with empathy to comprehend the words and actions of other people, and the reactions to those actions. This may cause pain in the person who suffers or be at times indifferent, depending upon whether the person has a need to be in an intimate relationship (such for people who have Asperger) or if it's indifferent.

3. Mind Theory Distorted Mind Theory

The concept of the mind is the capacity we have to comprehend that other people have their own thoughts as well as their own motivations and desires and that they could be different to ours. The absence of empathy could cause or contribute to an issue in this regard and there's an inability to distinguish one's personal perspective from that of other people may be thinking.

4. Egocentrism

The most common thing among people who lack empathy is that they view everything from their own viewpoint, believing they are the only valid point of view and not taking into account the validity of other perspectives. Also, there is the possibility of self-centeredness. The only or most important factor is what you want to defend your rights and success of your goals.

5. Narcissism

Although it's not mandatory but it is typical for those lacking the ability to feel empathy, to experience a level of narcissism. This includes thinking of them to be more valuable or superior over others and placing their own needs a priority over the rights of others. This issue is closely linked to the last issue.

6. Inadequacy of communication and context inadequacy

In conversation with others one who doesn't exhibit empathy is characterized by a communication style that doesn't consider or is not concerned about how other people react. This means that they are able to ignore the pragmatic aspects of language and transmit messages with extreme hardness with no tact towards the people they transmit. This may not be apparent in the event of attempts to manipulate when the person is of high intelligence and can be aware of how certain things affect other people.

7. Impatience

Another common characteristic of people who aren't emotionally connected is the lack of empathy for other people: they do not appreciate or understand the needs of other people and find it annoying to have to repeat or spend time doing things with others, and then integrating them.

8. Stereotypes and prejudices are a part of the process.

The lack of the ability to feel empathy is what causes individuals to rely on stereotypes and prejudices, operating at a cognitive level, and using labels to influence their thinking and behavior. They also are unable to discern how their actions affect the actions of other people.

9. Disruptive, superficial, or avoided relationships

One thing that is common to people who are lacking empathy is in the absence of being able to comprehend and consider the emotions and thoughts of others as valuable or fascinating and being unable to understand their own place, they typically keep relationships that are shallow and superficial relationships. It's possible that this kind of relationship is just cordial or there is a an enticing behavior that is designed to meet their needs or to be specifically avoided since they are unintelligible.

10. Utilitarian behaviours

Someone who has a severe lack of empathy is likely to use other people as a means to accomplish their goals. The inability to be capable of putting oneself in another's shoes makes the other person marginalized and glorified, using it directly or indirectly to achieve the goals of their own emotions.

11. Violence and aggression

While not all people with no empathy are violent (for example, those with autism may have issues with empathy but aren't generally violent) However, the reality is that the lack of empathy makes it easier for people to use solution-oriented approaches. Violence or aggression are a problem are when there is no understanding of the implications to the other person or the pain they may cause.

12. No regrets

Being hurtful to someone else typically causes regret in many people. In people who lack empathy regrets are absent or are much less however they might apologize if they've got the realization that others have been hurt or suffered, or if it is appropriate for them to fulfill their purpose.

The lack of empathy of the couple How does it affect us?

A lack of empathy within the relationship is a problem that can be detrimental to the relationship between the two in light of the fact that empathy is the capacity of individuals to imagine themselves in the position of another and feel their pain in a manner that is real. In other words, If you're compassionate you will experience the suffering of others like you, and empathize with the other.

In relationships with loved ones it is crucial for couples to be able to conquer the difficulties of emotional co-existence.

If the relationship is not able to show compassion within the love bond it can cause the relationship to become unstable, which can be detrimental for both parties.

On the other hand the one who doesn't feel compassion is in a position of vulnerability, as there is no one to talk to, regardless of whether another person is also with him as a relationship (technically) There is no genuine emotional connection. nor affective.

However, the person who is not compassionate is put in the position that causes emotional pain even if they do nothing to hurt or disrespect the other person in any way It is the inability to express emotion that causes harm.

In relationships, both partners should be emotionally connected so that the sorrow of the other is that of the other because of that emotional bond, you will be able to find the most effective solutions in a partnership.

If this empathy bond is not present in the minds of either or both parties, the relationship will end. If there is no empathy, certain relationships can be able to last for a while, but end in a bad way.

What can be done to resolve this problem in the relationship?

1. Be sure to consider the views of your companion

The link between empathy and compassion can develop from respect for each other A first step might be to consider taking into consideration the viewpoints of our partners. Don't just listen to them respond to you , but actively consider what you have to say to us.

2. Do not make Value judgments

A common error in relationships is the value judgements made by one of the participants and without any sort of support to make them. These kinds of unjustified opinions just serve to push the other away and cause distrust to the relationship. They should be avoided.

3. Cultivate patience

One of the virtues that must be maintained when it comes to relationships, especially during difficult situations, is patience. The ability to resist the temptation to say or act things at any given time will lead us to an empathy-based behavior towards one another that aids in communication. must promote patience.

4. Promotes understanding

We need to realize that we may not always be the right person and that it's sometimes good to allow our arms to turn when we're wrong. It is crucial to attain the ability to compress relationships and be able to observe the events as they happen rather than as we'd like them be.

5. Practice kindness

A relationship must be built on respect and affection among the people who form the emotional connection. Whatever jokes could be part of the context in the marriage, loving respect should always prevail in the dynamics of a couple. This is essential to build the state of empathy.

6. Make sure you are careful about how you speak to yourself

It's not the same to behave in a polite and calm manner, as to express it through shouting or yelling. This is also a component of the affection of the couple, but it is based on an assertive voice. It's not enough to simply speak, you must also be able to communicate them.

7. Peace is to achieve a goal

No matter what conflict is brewing, try to envision an outcome that could see everyone is at peace in both the context of the relationship as well as the level of individual. If you establish peace as the goal of the relationship you share, in time you'll be able to deal with the issue in a constructive and effective manner.

8. Bet on the honesty of your source

Sometimes, the absence of empathy may be due to the lack of love for another person. Sometimes it happens that couples remain in a relationship only because of their habit of being with each other.

How can you develop your empathy?

Learn to recognize your own emotions - build an emotional intelligence

We are often too "objective" or "controlled" about our feelings that it is difficult to recognize them within us, let alone others.

For instance, we could be able to confuse rational and analytical thinking with emotions. If someone asks you what you think about a task it is possible to respond pragmatically, "I think we have lots of work to accomplish." Instead of considering your feelings from the perspective of your emotions, feelings desire, frustrations and desires concerning the undertaking. It is possible that we are unable to differentiate between similar (similar) emotions such as separating anger from frustration or from exuberance. This is a major issue to be solved by regular debugging exercises, and an comprehension of our own emotions, as well as the emotions of other people.

Find out regularly from others about their opinions and perspectives about a particular situation.

Compare your answers to the answers you'd hoped you would get. This technique will not only help you develop your interpersonal skills but also allows you to learn more about your employees.

Inspire curiosity in strangers

People who are highly compassionate have an unstoppable interest in strangers. They'll chat with the person next to them at the station... These people keep the same curiosity we were as kids. They discover that other people are more interesting than they are However, they aren't willing to confront them, following the guidelines of oral historian Studs Terkel "Don't be an examiner, become the researcher who is interested."

How important is it in Our Daily Lives

Solidarity: It's a mistake to believe that this term is exclusively associated with volunteering. The ability to see others' understanding of your challenges and offering assistance whenever you require it and whenever you can is a great way to show your solidarity. Therefore, don't close your eyes from your friends or family members, as well as coworkers who require your assistance because of a need.

Respect: Recognizing that each person chooses their own path in life and recognizing this choice is essential for every human being. It is unfortunate that this isn't something that happens constantly around the globe, but it's not because of this that you cannot be courteous and kind towards anyone. Be respectful of your lifestyle choices and beliefs, sexual orientation, religion as well as political opinions as well as other issues that can create difficulties in the discussion. If people who are older didn't ask the things that make them different and the world would be more peacefully in the present.

Be aware of the essence Coaching teaches you how crucial listening to individuals in the essence.

That means you pay attention to what your counterpart has to say, integrate and accept it, then give your thoughts with respect. This type of conduct shows that you are interested in having everyone's views expressed within the appropriate space. This is a crucial aspect of the health of a discussion, isn't it?

Learning: You have to constantly evolve throughout your life. In order to do that, you shouldn't ever stop learning. Engaging with fellow professionals, interacting with others the latest research, reading, as well as pursuing courses that complement yours and coaching are ways to stay current and evolving regularly. Make sure to continue your education as well as different methods of learning.

Collective Awareness: Collectivity is crucial within the business world and also outside of these environments, as it is the key to a harmonious living in society. More than simply understanding how to work together The community also teaches us to respect the opinions of others and to be inclusive of all people, even people who have had less opportunities.

159

Chapter 14: Values

Your values form a huge element of what you're about. They determine what you think is right in the world both from yourself and other people. These are the principles that mean to you a lot and that you adhere to at the highest level. They can be extremely beneficial to your life and are something you admire.

The majority of people adhere to their beliefs with fervor and are unable to change their beliefs. People who are self-defeating might be more likely to abandon their beliefs or "let them go" in the event that a pushy person is encouraging it, because they don't think their beliefs are worthy of being a part of the conversation. It's not a moral flaw, but rather the inability to believe in yourself and to take good care of yourself in the way you want to. You're letting others control your life, which deprives your of the power you have been given and should exercise.

This is where the word "no" is crucial. Being able to say no is among the most essential abilities you can acquire in your daily life. The ability to say no frequently eludes those who have low self-esteem. You deserve to be respected for your personal boundaries and the only way you can earn this respect is by telling people to stop. Most people aren't aware of what the rules are, and even If they do, they'll continue to test the rules. The act of telling people no could anger them However, most of the time it only inspires them to respect your boundaries. You will notice a significant change in your daily life if you are able to stick to your beliefs and encourage others to be respectful of your boundaries.

Recognizing Your Values

Things that make you get up and makes your heart beat and that trigger an immediate and powerful reaction from you, these represent your values. If someone makes you feel humiliated and you feel he's breached your beliefs. Looking into what causes you to be angry will reveal what you value. Write down your beliefs in a diary to create clearer idea of who you really should be and how you want to defend.

It is worth looking over the sample values list below for a better understanding of what you stand for. Take a look at your political affiliations or religion, the way you are parenting, and how you manage your own children if they have any additional ideas. Consider what you are trying to bring to work and what you would expect from other people. Also, think about the moment where you were the most content and the actions you took to attain that level of joy.

An Example List of Values

If you're confused about what types of values you can be included, here's an example of the list.

Your beliefs could relate to religion, and in that the case they're equally relevant to the common personal and religious ideals that people share. Don't let others make you feel shameful or "weird" because you are religious. Your beliefs matter and should be honored. If you're a member of a religious group take note of the importance it holds to you, and the rules they require you to adhere to like treating your body as an altar or putting your ego aside.

Your ideals could depend on how you were taught. Maybe you were taught to be a woman or gentleman and hate it when people do not thank you for holding an open door or take out chairs for them. Your manners are something you value from your childhood. You might also be a feminist or maybe not.

The political values you choose to follow depend on the person you are as an individual. It's not unusual for children to be raised in a conservative home and then become liberal or the reverse. Your political views might not be based on your upbringing, but on the human values that you cherish in your heart. The political affiliation of your party will help you understand the values you value within the society.

Your values may also relate to ethics. People have a fundamental concept of the right and wrong. The ethics we adhere to are part of our society. The most fundamental are freedom of speech, appearing professional, looking presentable and keeping your business private by not chatting about it and not committing crimes like theft, adultery and murder. While these are values that are rooted in religion however, they are fundamentally American values that the majority of Americans have in common. The values may change depending on your country.

Other values that people believe in include:

Family time spent with the family

Nurturing children with love and love

Finding time to relax

Take care of your pets as if they were family

Animal rights

Being creative

Beauty

Accomplishment

Risks that are necessary

A healthy and nourishing friendship

Dating and romance

Treating others the way you would like to be treated

Working with other people

Feeling compassion

Forgiving others

Giving what you can to worthy causes or cause

Learn what you can

Being enthusiastic

Being courteous and polite

Smiles

Being kind to people

Respecting the rights of others

Be loyal to your family and friends as well as causes

Earning money

Working hard

Making a great impression the first time

First, peace.

Leave a clean Earth so that our future generations can enjoy a clean environment

Profit maximization

Happiness is the goal

Care for your body

Win

Being the best are able to be

The Best Way to Prioritize Values

Values define your goals and guide you to make the right decisions. So, they're always at the top of your list. Nobody can convince you that your beliefs are not right or suggest that you change them. There are many who will convince you otherwise and insist that you abandon your beliefs in favor of theirs, but they're wrong in their approach. Sticking to your own set of values and not letting them change is the essence of "prioritizing the values you hold dear." Your values should priority over the opinions of others are secondary.

Life is full when you live in accordance with your beliefs. You aren't feeling as satisfied when you perform actions in your life or work that you believe are wrong or when you don't agree with your actions. If you let others influence you to do actions that don't align with your ideals, you'll are numb and in a state of nausea. Believing in your values and putting your actions in line with your beliefs will allow you to live a healthy, balanced life that you are proud of. Your self-esteem will grow to the size of a balloon that is fueled by the helium that is your personal determination and self-confidence.

Understanding how you feel about your beliefs is the initial and most important step to determine the most effective way to lead your lives. If your career, studies or other activities do not align with your beliefs and beliefs, it is time to reconsider the things you do in your daily life. If your family, partner or even your friends pressure you to abandon your beliefs in favor of theirs, think about your relationships. People you love don't want to keep doing things you are not comfortable with.

If you know what your ideals are, you can be in touch with your inner voice. It will be difficult and frightened if you break your own morals. Learn to be able to say no when required to perform actions that cause you to feel a nagging feeling within your stomach. Let people know your personal rules and make clear the consequences for individuals violate those rules. It's fine to break relationships with those who are unwilling to accept and acknowledge your rules. It's also acceptable to quit a job which frequently requires you to perform things that do not align with your personal morality. Abusers and bullies often attempt to twist your thoughts to convince you that your beliefs are not right to get their ways with you, but when you place your values above everything else, you will be able to take on them and not be a victim of their snares.

Value prioritization can help to make decisions at times that are the most difficult. Naturally, life often requires us to make heart-breaking sacrifices or uneasy compromises. Make a list of the top 10 values you hold dear determine their importance in order of importance, starting with one being the most significant to ten being the least important. The most important value is family, while the second one is the pet of the family. You might find that paying for your dog's vet bill isn't enough to feed your child according to this ranking of values, so it can help you make an extremely painful and difficult choice. It's not an easy choice, but it's one that best aligns with your ideals.

Prioritizing your values will help you assess the people who are in your life, and also new ones who are entering the scene in your journey to create a positive environment. It also helps you take the garbage out, or so it's called. Pay attention to how people react to your values and whether they regard them. Pay attention when someone tries to dissuade you from own values, shams you by pointing out their values or doesn't respect the values of others. Anyone who offends your beliefs is a sloppy person in the truest sense. He'll savagely ruin your self-esteem and self-confidence to obtain what he wants and, once the time comes for him to stop using you and is done, he'll flit around, unharmed and satisfied and in search of the next victim.

Don't let yourself be weak. You are worthy of more. Eliminate the rude people and only invite people who are able to adhere to your beliefs. This doesn't mean you have to agree with all of your values , simply that they should be a decent human being, and not be a jerk to you. In general, however, people feel more comfortable with those who are the closest to them. You are likely to not enjoy a good relationship with someone who doesn't agree with your beliefs and has numerous things you find in off with.

The process of identifying your values is an enlightening and enriching aspect of the process of coming to know yourself. It's an experience that can help you to discover the person you truly are. However, as time goes by the conviction you have of your values can begin to weaken and diminish. That's why reviewing your beliefs at least every 6 months is a recommended step in this journey. List your top ten priorities in a pleasing manner and save the file on your computer or the treasure chest or other secure, personal space. Review them and pull them out the documents at least once a year.

However you could put your values prominently in places that you are likely to be able to see them, to remind you of them every day. This is a great idea if you're not worried about people seeing your values. You should not because you don't have anything to be embarrassed about. Your values are as important as another man's and aren't incorrect, regardless of the lies people try to tell you.

Insuring They Are Respected

Values are important.

How do you assess and enforce your beliefs

What are the values and why are they important?

Your values matter to confidence and self-esteem. If your lifestyle aligns to your ideals, you'll feel more satisfied, happier and content.

If your lifestyle does show your true values you'll be unhappy and uneasy and erode your confidence as a result. Your values can assist you make decisions and make better choices that can affect your mental, emotional and physical well-being.

Many people do not know the values they hold. In the end, they live the majority of their lives without the direction they need and no sense of purpose.

Values can be helpful in various areas of life such as:

What profession should you pursue?

Do you need to pursue a job?

Do you want to start your own company?

What kind of friends do you need to be able to

Are you ready to move into your new residence?

Are you ready to start a family?

Use these steps to discover your most important values.

1. Find the moments when you were the most happy

Include your personal and professional life, create your own list of times that you were most content. In the list, include details of the activities you took part in along with who you were spending time with and other aspects that contributed towards your joy.

Examples:

I was extremely content when my children were born and I was also with my husband.

I was extremely happy to receive an increase in my salary.

I was extremely happy to see to see my blood pressure drop to levels that were healthy.

2. Consider the times when you felt most satisfied

Also, taking into consideration your professional and personal life take note of times when you were confident. In the list, include details of the things you were of, the people who was proud of you and other aspects that led to your feeling of pride.

Examples:

I was very satisfied when I finished my college. I was very proud of myself when I graduated.

I was very satisfied when I managed to save enough money to purchase my first car.

I was extremely proud that my business had achieved its first revenue.

3. Find the moments when you felt most satisfied and fulfilled

In examining your professional and private life, pinpoint instances when you felt content and happy with your life. In the notes, describe how your you wanted or needed to be fulfilled the way these events gave you meaning in your lives, as well as which elements or people were responsible for satisfaction and satisfaction.

Examples:

Being in my home with family and friends makes me feel content and content.

My home is where I feel happy and content.

The fact that I have completed my workouts every week feels good and content.

4. Define your values of the most important to you.

With your list of options You should take a few minutes narrowing down your list to the items you think are the most significant. Try to reduce your list down to ten or less items.

There are also instances when there overlaps from one list on to the following. This is fine. Anything that makes you smile could be something that makes you feel content or happy. Actually, things that are on multiple lists include "hot item" which should be added to the cut on your essential values list.

It's also possible to combine the same values to create the concept of a "super value" therefore, if exercise brings you joy and you're happy with your physical appearance both of these items can be placed together.

5. Prioritize your core values

Here is the most difficult part of the exercise! Make your list and place them in order of importance. It may require a few attempts and you could discover that your values shift in accordance with the way you feel at the time. Make use of Post-it notes so that you can rearrange your values without revising them.

If you are trying to choose among two, or even more choices Consider what you would do if you had to pick one, which would you pick? It's the one that needs to be the top of your list. Repeat this process until you've got a final list.

6. Instilling your beliefs

Make sure you are demonstrating your values through this last exercise. It will ensure that your values match with your lifestyle and your goals towards the future. It can be done within the next day following the compilation of an inventory of the values you want to incorporate, so that you can look over your values using fresh eyes as well as clear thinking.

For each value, think about:

Are you comfortable enough to be able to share these values with your family, friends, or coworkers?

Are you proud of your beliefs?

Do you think about your values? Does it makes you feel better about you?

Even if these values suggest that you're part of the minority or cause you to be not popular, are they inviolable?

If yes, the value should remain in your mind and be considered a core value. If not it may not be as crucial in your opinion as you initially thought and should be relegated or removed off your checklist.

Once you've prioritized your goals, you'll understand what's crucial to you in your daily life as well as the goals you need to work towards, and what choices you'll need to make.

If, for instance, your family is among your main priorities, then a large portion of your choices in life should be focused on building and strengthening the family. If you're concerned about your health, then your fitness and diet plan should be top of the list.

When confronted with difficult choices and assignments, anxiety and self-doubt may hinder you from taking action. But, you might realize that what you must to do can bring you closer to fulfillment, happiness or fulfillment due to the fact that they directly affect the core values you hold dear to you. This will often be enough to assist you in overcoming the obstacles that you are facing.

Chapter 15: What Makes An Individual

Unprofitable?

There are a lot of articles written on the most efficient method of achieving success However, not many are addressing the elements that cause you to be unsuccessful! To be successful there are certain elements that you must be aware of to be successful. One of the components include:

False belief: Any incorrect belief you hold regarding something is deceitful.

The most important thing to do for growth is to let go of deceits by moving past them and advancing beyond. A small deceit such as being unlucky or unable to start a new line of work should not stop you from seeking work. To overcome deceits you must get out of the familiarity of their surroundings and be open to requirements with the intention to defeat their lies and move towards a fresher and more exciting future.

External Control: A particular viewpoint that is unambiguously linked to being ineffective is blaming all external components. For instance, when a person does not perform properly in a test they blame their teacher or even the natural environment surrounding the person. Whilethose who are successful go back to their own inner place of control, where they realize that they are accountable for every aspect of their life. They bolster themselves within to ensure of being able to tackle any challenges life throws at them.

Persistence and perseverance The successful generally remain steady all the time.

every day routine. They will generally go on through their daily tasks until they have achieved

What they want. In the event of trust deteriorating, these are the signs of those who do not stand up when they have failed. Therefore, be a strong and dependable person on the off chance you're hoping to achieve success.

Resilience: The people who fail tend to be rigid. They tend to stick to their old methods and aren't interested in adapting to changing circumstances.

In today's world of power it is essential to be flexible to be successful. It is essential to adapt to the changing circumstances make the most of hardships and test different strategies in the unlikely possibility of a failure.

Unskillful planning: Making arrangement for your life could assure you of success. If you are in charge of your own plans and you keep your focus and keep the correct direction. Some people who fail do not design, or the fact that they do the arrangement, it is fragmented. This is why you must be organized or you'll get cleared by those in your vicinity.

Insecurity: Have you wondered why the most successful are always abandoned?

It's all because of the manner in which they don't have the ability to express their thoughts to the supervisors. It is essential to shout your ideas, think outside the box and share your ideas with the intention of making your colleagues know that you're certain.

Thinking about the lack in assets. A good number of people who are ineffective are left behind due to the fact that they do not have enough funds or assets to accomplish their goals. What is the reason they are stalled? If you believe that you'll be successful it is essential to be able to complete your tasks without resources.

Fears: These aren't the trepidation or anxiety of the tiniest or tallest rather, they fears can impede your capacity to move toward advancement. Albeit

In the opposite, fear of disappointment or progress can hinder your path toward success, so overcome your fears of fear and get moving!

Conclusion

It's a skill can't be learned through the process of osmosis. It is possible to take this book and keep it on top of your head and you will never experience any change. Self-confidence will only be a reality in your life when you look for it and develop it. Also you must be able to act upon it. Don't sit around waiting for the moment to arrive "just perfect" to feel secure. You can't wait to start improving your confidence. You must begin today as tomorrow could become too late.

There's a good thing about it. that confidence is a lot easier than you imagine. Why? It's because you already possess something that you can trust. We all have our own passions. Everyone has interests. If we choose to pursue these interests and passions we can build our self-esteem. The more you are happy with yourself, the more you believe you're worth it, and the greater your self-image grows. Then, you can increase this until you are able to project it as confidence in your self.

Then, people immediately believe that you are aware of the way you're going. They then instantly believe they are able to believe in them. They think that you are convincing and this is due to confidence in yourself. The good thing is you have all the basic ingredients to create confidence in yourself. Nobody is an empty slate and do not have anything to build confidence. We wish all of you less than the best success.

CPSIA information can be obtained
at www.ICGtesting.com
Printed in the USA
BVHW052337090223
658265BV00032B/708